# The

# Rose

ISBN: 979-8-9861763-6-9

Cover Design by: Sherry Nelson

Developmental Editor and Editor in Chief:

Diane Novack

Managing Editor: Sherry Nelson

Publisher: Soul Professor Publishing

# Dedication

This book is dedicated to my children, the light in my world, the reason behind all I do. Your constant love and acceptance pushed me to heal and made this journey possible. Remember who you are. I leave this legacy and road map to aid you in your darkest moments and to remember how strong you are and where you come from. I love you.

\*\*\*

Sharing my life stories of addiction, family trauma, suicide, forgiveness, healing, spirituality, and the bravery it took to write about and relive the ugliness has been one of the most courageous things I have done.

My reason for taking on this difficult endeavor of writing about and sharing so much suffering is to show that a dark and painful story doesn't have to be a forever story. My desire is for others to find hope, forgiveness and courage so they too may find a way to change their story; by learning they have the power within to do so. This is a memoir from loss to fulfillment, broken to healed, lost little girl to warrior.

The pages of this book will shed light on each major moment in my life, my deepest wounds, and my darkest secrets. I want to be as vulnerable as possible, to help not only my children but many others who might be struggling to find the light within themselves. It is the reason I share my story.

# Acknowledgements

My children for loving me unconditionally, pushing me to become the best version of me.

My brother for always being my biggest supporter. Your constant love and support are everything.

My editor, mentor and friend Diane Novack for helping this book become everything I dreamed. You are truly a magical soul.

My second editor and artist Sherry Nelson for bringing the small details and beauty this book holds.

My boss and friend Jenny for allowing me to be me. Trusting me fully and giving me the space and time to write. Your acceptance has helped me in more ways than you can imagine.

My women of yoga who have supported me over this last 2 years and openly gave me the space to be me, loved and accepted me fully and showed me how special I am.

My therapist Renee for being the one who showed me this book was possible and helped me to figure out the loose ends on my path to healing.

Laura from yoga who magically appeared one day at class and introduced me to my editor Diane. Serendipity.

My spiritual team above, always cheering me on and giving me gentle nudges, guiding me along my path of healing. You never let me down and when you whispered, nudged or yelled I listened.

# Forward

"Becoming The Rose" was presented to me by Julie Andrews as her passion project to reveal to others how not accepting your current life and situation can lead you to the Divine Being you were designed to be. The level of courage shown within these pages is inspiring and for me greatly appreciated. There are many places where Julie could have glossed over the darkness of the situation, but she bravely chose to stay completely vulnerable knowing she could easily be judged by the reader.

She instead chose to lay out all the ugliness because of her underlying soul mission to help others see the light at the end of their own dark and scary tunnels. As Julie purged and healed through the release of writing her story, she changed and grew significantly, and the title morphed into "The Rose". Realizing she was no longer becoming, she had arrived.

Her journey has been extremely difficult. She has learned to push through the dirt, not stop because thorns have made her bleed, to keep going, keep learning, keep growing. Now the blossom of her true self has been revealed. You, the reader, are invited to use this road map showing there is a way to grab the Spirit-led opportunities and change the trajectory of your life.

As Julie shows, no one can do that for you, no one is coming to save you, you have everything you need within yourself. It has been a true honor to assist in this life altering book.

Love, Light and Peace, Diane Novack Six-time Amazon bestselling author Assistant and Guide to those learning to find their voice by telling their stories. Editor Publisher.

# Table of Contents

*"The journey from pain to healing is like the unfolding of a rose—slow, deliberate, and touched by both shadow and light. But within every struggle lies the seed of transformation, waiting for the moment we dare to bloom."*

# Part One

# The Seed

*"Beneath the frost, a seed will rest*

*Unseen, yet yearning, it's quiet quest*

*The Rose reminds, in its gentle grace*

*That beauty emerges from the hardest place"*

You are holding an unfiltered and vulnerable story of facing addiction, suicide, abandonment, working with the pain and using it to my advantage for healing. You will go on the journey with me of understanding why it happened, understanding that everything "happened for me, and not to me." You will learn how Little Julie found a way out of being a victim of the trauma and has now become a warrior battling her way out of the dark and into the light. I will share how digging deep into Little Julie's dark underworld and facing it allowed Me, Big Julie, to accept myself fully for who I was and now am. I now know the dark and ugly parts I tried to ignore became my most valuable parts.

I have come to an understanding of how my Guides protected me, which allowed me to survive over the years. When I was able to look back, I unmasked the truths of Spirit from which Guides function—always working for our highest good, even when it may not seem that way at the time.

I learned to love the dark side of me and to understand who I really am underneath it all. That internal work brought me to many realizations. The most profound is that forgiveness is the key to unlocking the victim mentality, releasing me from my pain and trauma. By incorporating forgiveness for yourself, you too can begin to heal. Understanding and forgiving myself for all the wrong I created over the years released my trapped soul from the unfathomable bondage that surrounded me in repeated cycles of dysfunction. This allowed me to understand that everyone is human, and is going through their own pain, darkness and trauma. It allowed me to feel others' pain, and understand they are only living the way they have been taught, just like I had been doing. We only live the way we are raised until the moment in our lives we become conscious of the truth: that we are destined to be free rather than stuck in those reoccurring and reopening wounds.

You will likely judge me, probably not like me and think all kinds of things, but my reasoning behind telling my story is to help my children and anyone who is ready to start facing the unfathomable things that happen in your life.

I have laid out and shown my most vulnerable parts through these pages with the hope it helps just one person see there is so much more than what we think we have been dealt, and the minute one seed is planted the rose can begin to grow. This book is titled "The Rose" for more than one reason. The main being the song "The Rose" by Bette Midler was my mother's favorite song when I was little.

I remember her playing this song over and over watching the tears fall down her cheeks. This song forever sticks in my soul, mind and heart and every time I hear it, I get transported right back to those feelings of longing to be free, to feel loved, to feel like a rose that has bloomed on the first day of spring. All the things my mom longed for but never got. Her life was cut way too short, leaving a little girl and boy whose lives were turned upside down in a blink of an eye. The long winding road and journey to becoming "the rose" is what you will find within my story.

Most people are afraid of change and remain in repeating cycles because it is actually easier than doing the hard work of facing our dark shadow parts. The less scary road: the safe road is to stay where you know the familiar, even when the familiar is awful. Hence, the reasoning behind addiction: this is what I know and am comfortable with therefore I can get through the day living my addiction rather than taking on the uncharted changes that MIGHT help. Notice that capital word. That is the deep unknown; will hard work, a different lifestyle, maybe losing all my friends really make a difference? I have done so many bad things, there is so much to change, can I even overcome all that? Shame, and guilt that comes with the repeated trauma you live through, and cause, gets stronger and deeper, and it gets intensely difficult to see redemption of any kind, so you continue to dig your hole deeper causing more suffering to yourself, and others, feeling stuck and unworthy of love, and or forgiveness.

Then the wisdom of your soul begins to whisper to you. Quietly at first, then as years pass the whispers become louder and louder, illuminating all the dark places needing attention and you start to listen, awakening something inside. The more you listen, the more you seek, the more your soul speaks, you become ready.

The whispers plant seeds of what could be; that you are designed to be much better. As the whispers become more distinct messages, all the seeds planted over the years begin to burst through the muddy dark soil of your world into a beautiful sprouting of life, yearning for the light, love and nurturing that comes when you are ready to bloom. Opening each petal slowly, releasing each part of yourself that you deemed broken, unlovable, guilty, hated, judged and unforgiveable.

You began to free yourself from the learned bondage as you dedicate time, desire, new actions and allow a different pattern to appear. You begin giving yourself the love you always craved from the outside. The internal love that has always been there, just hidden, is now given solely to yourself, for as long as it takes. Believe me, it took many years from my first spiritual awakening to get to where and who I AM today.

I am sure more pain appeared in my life by choosing my will over my soul's knowing. It took getting to my final bottom place to open my eyes and be ready to listen fully and allow my soul to take the reins moving me into the place I reside currently.

A kind of freedom of sorts came over me. My inner peace is reflected as outer peace now. A once distant world my soul longed for is now my reality and I feel safe within this space, which allows me to share my story with you in hopes it will plant a seed of hope and begin your soul's journey to becoming The Rose.

Our stories create the outline and narrative of our lives, but we have the power to change it at any time. Our stories are our greatest ally, and we become either a victim or a warrior. Through these pages I take you on a journey of a soul whose destiny was much greater than her fate.

Through completed and attempted suicides, physical, mental and sexual abuses, addictions, unplanned terminated pregnancies and much more, my life taught me hard lessons. I was taken to places I didn't think I could recover from.

In those times I could never fathom my life could be so peaceful.

All my life I was programmed to believe life is hard, full of disappointments, pain and tragedy. I was a survivor; always, in a fight or flight mode, never thinking that happiness was available to me. I am here to tell you that is not true. The story of survivor Julie is over, done, and I am now living a peaceful life, full of magic, miracles and happiness.

I am sure you are saying to yourself, how is this possible? Is there a chance I can live this type of life too? I can assure you the answer to these questions is YES. Through many life lessons, connections, pain, and loss, I have discovered that the power to attain a peaceful life was always in my hands. It was inside of me. The answers I sought were always right there, within me. Which is kind of ironic because that is the last place most people would look.

Everyone wants to seek happiness outside of themselves, in a Magic Pill; believing if someone, or something could heal the pain they would be happy. Seeking that bigger house, a better relationship, relief through drugs and alcohol is easier than looking inside at the reasons behind the pain we have endured and how we might change those learned patterns.

The wounds are our roadmap to all the magic the universe has to offer. It took me thirty-six years to obtain the first piece of the Divine puzzle of my life. Up to age thirty-six was such a mess, full of shit and it had me believing I was cursed or damaged and happiness was unattainable. I felt cheated and lost.

In this part of my life my actions were horrible, and my babies suffered with me along my journey. They also felt abandoned by me because I just didn't know how to be a mother. I had been a survivor since age ten, and that was the only person I knew how to be at the time.

This is a story of healing and getting to the other side of pain. Becoming a warrior is not easy, it is difficult, painful, and downright the hardest thing you will ever do in your lifetime. But staying stuck, stagnant in your life, repeating cycles, waiting for permission to become your new self, continuing patterns and pain over and over again, is the end result if you don't fight, if you don't become that warrior. It was my soul that refused to stay stuck.

Little nudges and whispers came early on and kept knocking at my internal compass, growing and becoming louder so that over time I had no choice but to listen, open that door and allow my soul to take over. My life got harder and harder until this happened. My greatest downfall, my rock bottom turned out to be the greatest awakening of my life.

If I can help to loosen the hinges of those doors and boxes you have been placed behind and in, my wish for you is granted. As you allow my story to inspire you to start listening to your soul, notice the whispers and nudges from the universe and begin the long road to healing. This book is about learning to come home to yourself, love yourself, forgive yourself, forgive others, open the wounds that hold you trapped in a world of suffering and pain.

Learn to create the life you are entitled to and deserve. Listen to my words, see how I was guided towards the inner work that was needed and allow my story to inspire you. I promise even the slightest shift in your perspective will allow the universe to start aiding you on your healing journey.

My childhood until age nine was typical, at least I thought so. I remember always playing, getting into everything, not being afraid of anything, I think trouble could have been my middle name I was so carefree with no fear, the "wild child" as my brother would say. He always said he hated me when we were young. I think it was due to me being so much younger than him. I was immune to the dysfunction, while he lived right in the middle of it. Living in my own world was my protection.

We moved often, which I think caused a lot of underlying anxiety and uncertainty. Through years without stability, I learned to keep the feelings of being out of balance and in constant fear well hidden by always being busy, playing and I guess you could say running. My brother is six years older than me and had a totally different experience. His early childhood was full of similar but different kinds of trauma, being an outcast and in pain. We had the same mother but different fathers. Around the time I was born, my dad officially adopted him. His dad was never in the picture when we were young, and his whole world was consumed by our mom being depressed and dependent on our dad. I was oblivious in my playful little world, but my brother suffered through the mental abuse of deep disfunction.

I never realized the pain he endured until I was older. He struggled with being accepted not only by my dad but our mom too. Her pain washed down on both of us, but the desertion of his father was a big reason for her feelings of unworthiness and guilt. By

11

association, my brother was the flesh and blood reminder of her trauma. Being older and more aware, my brother saw firsthand how depressed our mom was, how my dad cheated on her, plus he felt the pain of never being fully accepted in the family unit. In his words, Dad was "horrible" to him. My heart aches for the trauma he endured. We both suffered immensely in our childhood but through this trauma we have an unbreakable bond.

My brother was my whole world at age six. Oh, how I loved him. A fond memory I have from this time is the two of us sitting on our dark brown velvet sofa, with the Persian rug hanging on the wall behind us. We were probably playing records on the record player. This was one of our moms' favorite things to do. He is at one end of the couch, I on the other. I look at him and as serious as a six-year-old could be, I say "when I grow up, I am going to marry you, live in a big house and drive a pink Barbie corvette." I honestly don't remember what he said, but the fact this memory remains with me all these years shows the devotion, connection and love I had, and still have, for him. He was so funny and kind. Maybe underneath it all I did know the pain he struggled with and was showing him love as I could at that age. In this moment, my life was perfect, not knowing what the future would hold for us both. The blissful moment of this memory, still frozen in time and locked away in my mind would soon turn into terror and unbelief and our lives could never be this carefree with six-year-old romance again.

Abruptly the carefree life I was living changed. My mom was gone (hospitalized) for a nervous breakdown. Before I knew what was happening, life became a blur, and everything seemed to happen so fast. Dad moved my brother and me into a house with a whole new family. Later I found out my dad had been having an affair for three years with a woman he worked with. This was the main reason behind my mom's depressive state and continual breakdowns.

His new girlfriend and her two kids were mean and abusive. The kids were much older than me, and all I can remember about them was their dislike, maybe hatred of me, and my new stepmom was the devil in disguise. Classic story, right?

Adding to Mom's sad story, my dad finally filed for divorce, asking for full custody of my brother and me. We had to go before the judge and state who we wanted to live with. I pleaded to be allowed to live with my mom, and so did my brother. Our requests were ignored. Full custody was awarded to our dad, and my brother and I were devastated. Somehow, we knew there would never be another chance to change the ruling and live where we longed to be. This final loss and betrayal broke her that summer. Shortly after that final court date my mother decided she couldn't stay in her pain any longer. She was a lost soul, who suffered extreme pain because of my father's actions.

***

It was September 25, 1980. A day I will never forget. A day that would impact my entire life. It was the day my mother committed suicide.

At that time, in the moment, I didn't realize the impact that day would make. How could one, especially a child, know and understand what ripping your heart and soul in half would mean? The scar it made has lasted my entire life.

I was ten years old, the weather was beautiful, the beginning of fall, but still summer. I was outside playing not caring about anything, I was a happy Little Girl for a glorious moment. Little did I realize my whole world was about to change forever.

I was waiting for my dad to give me his answer about me playing the flute when he called me inside.

After attending music class at school, I fell in love. I was deeply drawn to the music and especially the flute. That little instrument made such beautiful noise and spoke to my soul. I wanted to play it more than anything. I went home and asked Dad if he would pay the school for lessons and allow me to play. When he called me into the house, I went skipping in with anticipation. I was sure his answer would be yes, and I would get my flute soon. He asked me to sit on his lap because he had something to talk about. I trembled with excitement. The words that came out of his mouth were not about the flute and will echo in my mind forever.

"Julie, I have something to tell you about your mom. Your mom had a heart attack, and she is no longer with us." "What? What do you mean, she is no longer with us?" My little brain could not comprehend those words. The still lingering thought of getting the flute overshadowed his words. I guess telling me Mom had a heart attack instead of the truth of suicide was his way of protecting me as best he could.

I laughed and said "Stop it. Stop playing with me. Am I getting the flute today?" He said again, "Julie, I am serious, your mom is dead." My whole world stopped in that moment. I froze and stopped thinking about my flute as I tried to process what I was just told. I couldn't think. I didn't understand.

I was in shock, I guess. I became numb, retreating inside myself and not coming out of that horror and trauma until years later. I remember going back outside, telling my friends "my mom just died," in denial, I guess. My young brain, heart and soul had just been broken. It took a long time for me to even comprehend what Dad's words truly meant. My life and the lives of my current stepfamily went on. The fact that we could all just keep doing the things we were doing before Mom died made comprehension even more difficult. There was no talk about how we felt, no counseling, just the cold hard fact that I would never see her again.

For many years I blamed him for her death. I carried that judgement and grudge for most of my life and his. I hated my dad. I hated living with him. He was a mean, hard and nasty man who seemed to care for only himself. I was terrified of him. I despised his girlfriend, her kids and my life as a whole at that time. Circumstances forced me to grow up fast without healthy role models, without basic care and nurturing. I became my own custodian at age eleven. Mom's death catapulted me deep into an extremely dysfunctional life. I am fortunate to have survived.

Just nine months earlier Mom's father, my favorite and only grandpa died. I believe the impact of losing her father played heavily in my mother's death. Their deaths happening so close together was too much for a little girl and I was broken. My grandpa was an alcoholic. I only have a few memories of him, but I loved him dearly and wasn't aware of his alcoholic traits. He always gave me coins and shared popsicles with me when I saw him. I adored him and I am glad I never knew the ugly side of him.

Mom's death was surreal, although I didn't know that word at the time. The week before she died, she came to the house and picked me up, which was very odd, but no one thought anything about it. She never just stopped by like this and I often wonder if only one person would have thought to ask her how she was doing, it might have changed things for her.

We went to Del Taco and had a meal together. I don't remember what we talked about. What I can tell you is I had a taco and was happy she was with me. I loved my mom and cherished her. She was so beautiful, and she loved and always played the best music on her record player. My fondest memories were just that, playing music, singing, dancing and being happy with her. I never knew she struggled with bipolar depression and nervous breakdowns. My family kept that from me, or I was living in my own world and I never paid attention. Later in life I learned from my grandma a bit about how difficult Mom's life really was. She always had a hard time living on her own, away from her mom, and suffered from various mental and emotional complications.

My dad was not the best husband and cheated on her multiple times, which only added to her pain and suffering. My brother saw more of this side of her which caused much pain for him. I got to witness firsthand what generational trauma and wounding is. Mom loved Dad more than anything in life, but according to my father her extreme mood episodes took a toll on him. She would attempt suicide to get him to come home and be with her. When they separated, then divorced, and her entire family left, I believe she experienced the greatest and final pain and could never be happy again.

*** 

Over the next year I went from a carefree little girl living a fun innocent life to my whole world, as I understood it becoming an absolute nightmare.

I stopped having fun and became a lost little girl with anxiety. Very quickly the wounded Lost Little Girl would be nourished more than any other part of me. Another new school, making new friends and the horror inside my new home life was just about to begin.

My new stepbrother and sister were older than me and they more than picked on me, they tortured me. I was separated from the family unit and not loved by them or my stepmother. She shunned me, made me do all the chores, and really made me feel unloved. I tried to stay unseen, by always being outside, playing and not at home. I hated being there in the house with them. My dad, not knowing how to make up for what he did, and to establish a false image of what a family looked like, tried to buy our love and family bond with horses and a nice house with a pool. I now believe the big house, pool and horses was how he tried to show we were a successful happy family, making himself feel better and apologizing to me in his own strange way; maybe the only way he knew how. I am sure the guilt was eating him up inside slowly because the path he would soon choose would be the one that destroyed my once innocent life.

My brother only lived with us for a short time. Memory of this time is foggy for both of us, probably because of survival mode repression. We tried to get the timeline down on when he actually moved away from this mess, but it is a hazy time for us. I only remember him being here for a very short time. I am grateful he was able to escape but I know he was dealing with his own nightmare. He eventually moved in with his father, and it would be many years before I would see him again.

I felt alone and my best escape was being outside as I said before. The strangers living in my world now not only abused me physically, but emotionally and my stepbrother sexually molested me. I pushed all this down as deep as I could by telling myself "This is normal, other families must act like this." Being outside more than in the house was a way to escape for a while and if I had to be inside, I locked myself in my room for safety. There are a few fond memories; one of playing records on my record player like I used to do with my mom and brother. I would sing and dance my worries away. That was my flight response avoidance at the time.

Living in the big house, having horses and other material things gave the outside appearance of a happy, normal family life while in reality everyone was dying on the inside. As best as I can recall this went on for about a year. In self-preservation and as a coping mechanism I blocked out a lot of what really happened during this time. What was about to happen next would take the front seat in my life.

During this time my dad started dabbling in drugs like cocaine and swinging with his new girlfriend. Yes, him and my stepmom became swingers. They moved us into a nudist camp which later would be their downfall, taking me down with them.

This was a period of being seen but not heard while he was living his best life. I honestly don't think he knew half of what was really happening in the household. From the sexual abuse of my stepbrother, physical and emotional abuse from my stepsister and HER, the evil stepmom.

He was blinded by her. His lust for her and the life they were living took over caring about what I was going through. I just remember not ever being able to talk to him or go to him for protection. He terrified me. During this time, he was strict, I would say over strict with everything. He had rigid rules and getting good grades was at the top of the list. My grades were not good so that meant I was often in trouble. When I didn't comply with his attempt to control, a severe spanking with the belt followed. I guess that is another reason I was always outside. The rebel in me was headstrong and more often than not I was in trouble. Staying outside, away from him and his new family as much as possible, kept the belt away and me safe from other abuses. Early in life I began to learn I didn't like rules, wanted to push back and if I separated myself then consequences were less (or so it seemed at that young age). Life gave me lessons of severe consequences later.

Not surprising, school was not my friend. I hated it. There were many rules I didn't care to follow, and it was extremely challenging. Moving often meant I was forced to try and find new friends over and over again. Feeling awkward and alone wore me down and kids figured out early I was an easy target. Struggling with grades, which were most important to dad at that time, my self-esteem and worth suffered. I was awkward socially because I hadn't learned how to make friends. Everyone faces inevitable trials of school. For me there was no safety net of social groups, or friends to share things with and my family was not a safe place to talk about not being perfect and the issues of not fitting in. I was one hundred percent alone, never being accepted by others. I remember early on being made fun of for so many things. A vivid memory of a second-grade class project is still with me. The assignment was: make a poster board of your family and go before the class to describe it. I was absolutely terrified to do this. It ended up being one of the worst days of my life and the wounds have stuck with me. I walked to the front of the class, shaking and barely able to breathe, as ready as I could be to reluctantly share my board. When I turned around to face the class, a boy who was a class bully was staring right at me. It felt like his eyes were boring a hole through me. The time I had been dreading was here. I tried to talk. All of the air silently left my lungs. Darkness seemed just on the edge of overtaking me. My mouth opened but there were no words. Nothing came out. I stood there with my silent gaping mouth. All eyes were on me, and I began to hear laughter. The bully, whom I was most terrified of, said something that caused me to cry, and the laughter got louder. I broke. I had to get out of there. RUN my brain screamed. Throwing the poster to the floor I ran crying. The laughter, judgement, fear and disappointment followed me through the door. I feel that day in my body as I write. The memory of horrible judgement, laughter and ridicule, is still in my body, not allowing me to speak in front of a group of people. I believe that day ripped a part of my soul out and I am still trying to face that fear and heal. Public speaking to this day is one of my fears I have yet to overcome. The scar on my soul and psyche only became bigger and bigger as I got older, manifesting itself in so many ways.

Not having support of any type, I was on my own to try and recover. Hence, the victims started to appear. My Lost Little Girl learned to adapt to all the different surroundings we found ourselves in and become someone she thought everyone would like. Chameleon Julie started to develop. She was able to not be seen, be invisible and less likely become a target. The Rebel who lived in my soul made great friends with Victim, and Lost Little Girl. Lost Little Girl receded further into the background while the others thrived and made decisions. The Survivor began to emerge slowly as each traumatic event unfolded in my life.

The world I lived in seemed to be always spinning and there was no one to anchor my little eleven-year-old self to. Still reeling from Mom's death and being in a horrendous abusive family while trying to understand what was happening in my life. The only stabilizing force and every little bit of safety I felt left with my brother when he moved with his dad. Bitterness was already a huge part of my life even though I didn't know how to express myself, let alone my emotions.

B ecause we moved often, it was very difficult to feel safe, I had no roots, there was no security. Making friends which builds confidence and strength didn't happen for me.

Soon life took an even more inconceivable course. Dad and my stepmom moved us into a nudist camp. I clearly remember that first day of horror. What was considered my family piled into the car. Sitting in the back seat with the two people who tormented me most, it felt like I was riding into the lion's den. In a way I was. It was here that Rebellious Julie grew and thrived so we could survive.

The only form of protection I had during the car ride was to fold my trembling arms across my tiny heaving chest and simply stare out the window. Driving through unfamiliar streets all I knew was each minute in the car was bringing us closer to another new place to live. I felt utterly and completely alone because my brother had just left. Suddenly the view from the window changed, the car slowed. My breathing got even more shallow and I could feel an invisible hand squeezing my heart. Before the car came to a halt, I got a first glimpse into the horror of the next two years of my life. The car stopped. I couldn't move. My ears rang with the throbbing of my quickly beating heart. With wide confused eyes I just stared at the property we were on. The sights were beyond my young scope of knowledge. I wasn't even sure what I was seeing. Nude people were everywhere.

I remember hesitating, not wanting to move, scared and wondering what the hell was happening. My dad said "get out of the car now. Go have a look around." After pondering my situation for a second or two, I decided to get out and the first thing I saw was a big pool, a clubhouse, a jacuzzi and lots of nude people. I was not conscious of taking my clothes off. This might be the first time I experienced disassociation. Suddenly I am aware of being naked and swimming, not giving a care. Disconnecting and disassociation became the way I was able to adapt and survive life's conditions and situations from this point on.

Little did I realize, there was no way I could at such a young age, this nudist camp's main purpose was for swingers to meet and freely exchange sexual partners as they chose. It was shocking to say the least. My young brain was conflicted by feelings of dread, curiosity, loneliness, contempt, disbelief, panic, confusion, denial and so much more. I did what I always did at that age to fit in as best I could and move through the days without too much confrontation. It was easiest to just accept it and lose myself in all the activities.

We had the large pool and jacuzzi that first greeted me, gardening, kids crafts, cooking, game nights and general kid play that happens when children gather. I was learning to put my fears, pain and thoughts into a box on a shelf and Chameleon Julie was our go to again. Living there was not all bad, I met my best friend at that nudist camp. I have to be honest; I did have a lot of fun living at the nudist camp, due to my bond with my best friend and her family.

Going through grades five and six was horrendous though; being made fun of because we lived in the camp. That only added more trauma to my experience with school. At least for these two years I finally had a friend who knew exactly what I was going through because she lived in the same place. We had each other and she was the first friend in school I had. We depended on each other, and I felt relatively safe with her by my side through this dreadful time with all the nastiness children could spray. I can't imagine going through that time without her, she was my rock.

Life was ruled by the obsession of being seen but never heard. I ran away figuratively and emotionally but not physically, yet. I felt safer within myself than with anyone else. Dad was my only true family, but he still terrified me and there was no real relationship with him. My stepmom was mean and getting meaner as time went by. I understand now her lashing out at me was partly because she wanted to hurt my father, she was suffering in her own way. The sting of unworthiness washed over me watching her kids get the best of what we had, and I was left out, again.

Chores were put on me, my stepbrother and sister had no responsibility around the house. I felt rejected and wanted to be alone in safety. That may be why I have such a keen sense of fairness as a healthy adult. When I finally stopped running away from the emotional pain and scars, I began to be able to use that pain to my advantage.

Thankfully, I didn't realize what was going on behind closed doors at home and throughout the camp until I was older. Carrying that burden also at that time would have caused even more shame and vulnerability, I believe. Life was screwed up enough for me, Little Girl was buried deep within, close to lost. I know there was trauma caused by this two-year moment in my life, but the word or idea of trauma wasn't in my consciousness. I had one therapist tell me it was a form of child molestation and abuse to me by simply living in that environment. Although living in the nudist camp had its own form of stress, pain and upheaval, I did not experience direct sexual abuse because we lived there but my stepbrother continued to fondle and sexually abuse me as he had when we lived the 'perfect life' in the house we had left.

Dad and my evil stepmom; picture the Cinderella story; finally separated. They ended up leaving each other for the couple they were swinging with, the woman would become my next stepmom.

I will never forget the day my dad left that evil woman, and he made me say goodbye to her. I went in her room, she was laying down, and said, "I hate you; I have always hated you, goodbye." It felt good. I remember being happy for a moment and ready for our move.

The short elation to leave that evil family soon switched to me thinking "Here we go again." Another move, another stepmom and I felt myself dissolving into a shell of someone who was scared to death.

Alone. A new town. A new school. Lost again, not knowing how to cry out for help or even who to ask.

When I was older, I found out my grandmother and great-grandmother both breathed a sigh of relief with me when we left. They were alarmed and in deep anguish when they found out I was living in a nudist camp. I never saw or consciously felt their distress about it but years later my grandma told me how devastated Great-Grandma was. Grandma felt the stress of us living in the nudist colony led to her mother's dementia, most likely causing her health to decline, eventually leading to her death. Great-Grandma was in a convalescent hospital for many years before her passing. I remember a small number of times I visited her there, and she really was not on this plane anymore. She didn't recognize me or grandma, her daughter.

It was heartbreaking to see her this way, because she had been such a solid haven for me until I was ten. I was so happy that I got to stay with Great-Grandma. There were fun days when she took my brother and me to the local plunge. It was a community pool, and as I mentioned before I loved swimming and so did my brother. When I stayed with her, it was an escape. She played with me and took me to her quilting groups at her church which was a blast. I would get the keys to every church room and play for hours by myself. I loved teaching imaginary students whatever my little mind dreamed of. She taught me how to sew, type on an old typewriter and loved taking me to watch the trains. These were good times. She was genuine and strong and that is what I needed most. I knew she loved me.

Great-Grandma lived across the street from a roller rink, and I spent many days there too. She told the most amazing stories of her life, in great detail. We would lay in bed at night laughing and singing songs. I owe a lot of great memories to her dedication and the love she gave me. She showed me love, and what love felt like. I am so thankful I had those few years with her before the camp. Sadly, Great-Grandma passed in 1987 when I was seventeen.

***

We left the nudists with stepmom number two. She was what I thought of as fancy, wearing elaborate clothes and enjoying fine things. That alone intrigued dad and I admit it was exciting to be in what felt like a better life, until I realized it wasn't. The same patterns of separation and neglect moved with us into a nice two-story house, the nicest house I have ever lived in; only to stay a year. Living in a beautiful house while taking up as little space as possible was easier when no one expected eye contact or had demands of any kind from me. All that was expected was for me to be quiet and stay out of the way. Feeling hollow inside, I found ways to avoid the adults and hide in plain sight. Except for a nicer place to live, it was like all other years so far but with no physical abuse. As I got more and more practice making myself small, covering up the pain and emptiness and keeping quiet it even became easier to stop holding my breath in hopefulness. To my father, school was most important. It felt as though all his hopes and dreams hinged on how I moved through school. I don't even know if he was aware of the bullying, name calling and terror I endured with

28

drooped shoulders and stomach aches, pretending the neglect and verbal abuse didn't matter. Between his unanswered expectations, the labels and increased bullying in seventh grade, I was a tight-lipped disappointment at home and verbal whipping post in school. Stepmom was all about Dad, and if I could disappear, sometimes I tried to will myself to do just that, she would have been happy. This period continued the spiral downward for my father.

Before I knew it my dad left her, and we moved to a small mountain town about seventy-five miles from Los Angeles. The area was beautiful but at twelve years old it was hard for me to appreciate or enjoy as I was again left alone, this time in a tiny two-bedroom cabin. Dad worked far away, would leave for the week, not coming back until the weekend. I met my second important best friend from that uncomfortable lonely cabin, and we became inseparable. Our parents were messed up and we were left to our own devices. He was my world, and I was his, there was a lot for us to bond over.

Between the ages of thirteen and fourteen I started partying a lot. It began when dad gave me marijuana. I quickly and easily became a pot head, getting stoned at the bus stop, school and home. I needed to escape and just numb myself from the bullying at school, and pain of living with the fact that no one seemed to give a shit about me. This eventually led to drinking and dropping out of school at the end of ninth grade. Being forced into early adulthood, taking care of myself and being on my own without guidance, I grew up sexually and lost my virginity that year. Self-loathing and anger led to outward signs that separated me; I would not, could not meet anyone's eyes, feeling the constant trembling inside, convinced others could see me shaking even though I wore baggy clothes covering every inch of my body, even my hands. The bullies recognized an easy mark and swarmed. There was so much fuel for them.

On top of all the reasons kids picked on me, was the absolute embarrassment of being known for giving myself away. I later discovered what that truly meant. I came to realize it's not just about the physical act of sex; it's about losing a spiritual and emotional part of yourself if there is no true connectedness with the other person. Even when you don't understand this part, it still happens and will in some way lead to a certain amount of brokenness and pain that will rear its ugly head at some point.

The feelings of worthlessness were already present, you could see that on the outside. My entire body and emotions were turned inside. With shoulders hunched and rounded, I kept my hands in my pockets and was always looking away, avoiding confrontation of any kind as best I could. There was no need or desire to make eye contact, I had no one that liked me and no reason to step out of my insulating little bubble that I hoped would protect me in some way. Everyone knew my dad, the drug dealer. No one knows the embarrassment and deep emotional pain of being the local drug dealer's daughter unless you have been. I didn't speak to anyone but my best friend. Constantly clinched teeth, the tightness in my chest, racing heart and overwhelming desire to run, just escape, wouldn't allow speaking to anyone else even if I had wanted to. No one would associate with me, except my best friend with whom all my self-protecting barriers were down. With him I was relaxed and felt safe enough to talk. We shared all the F-d up stuff about our parents, how school sucked and how we were going to get high.

The summer before what should have been my Sophomore year in High School, my dad offered me cocaine and I loved it. Cocaine turned into meth, and I thought I found what life was all about, I felt on top of the world.

Suddenly dad got laid off and wasn't working anymore. This is the beginning of the end for the man I once feared. He lost himself and became the local drug dealer and my first pusher.

I watched my father give up on life. He was teaching me how to be an adult. Our world consisted of drugging, partying, and staying up for days, not having any responsibility at all. It was okay to drop out, become a druggy and party with my father. When I turned fourteen, my dad was busted in a raid at the neighbor's house. I used this as an excuse to say "Fuck You" to him, steal his truck and dope and run away. My best friend and two other friends hopped in the truck, and we left the mountain with Los Angeles in our sights. What seemed like a fun independent way to leave that situation, became a life-changing time filled with terror, uncertainty and pain.

At the tender age of fourteen I lived as a street kid or in and out of group homes until I turned eighteen. I say tender age because it certainly is for all children. A child of that age should be in a safe and stable home where the only worries were choosing what to wear that day, whether or not to do homework and the like, and I knew that, but that wasn't where I was. No one, especially a child, should be exposed to life-changing, sometimes life-threatening daily terrors while trying to survive on their own. Children should be in a stable and safe home where they are fed, cared for and loved. I can honestly say I am not sure which was worse, the streets or the group homes.

The streets were day-to-day fear. Hours each day were spent pan handling and trying to find friends who could take me in for the night and feed me. Each and every day was full of terror and the nights were worse because very bad things happened at night. The questions were endless: where would I sleep tonight, would I be able to eat today, could I stay safe? Often the answers were: today I would not eat, maybe I can sleep in bits in a relatively safe corner on super alert. Sometimes it was better to keep moving; roaming from street corner to street corner, staying within the relative safety of streetlights trying to walk off the bitter cold that gripped me, hoping to find someone who would share what little food they had.

The relative safety of my dad's truck ended abruptly; it was repossessed while I was at a punk show in Long beach. I went outside and it was gone. I was devastated. Shortly after that, I was on the streets of Seal Beach and met a boy who soon became my world. Mark this as one of the bad decisions made concerning male companions. When someone pays attention when others haven't seemed to even notice you, there is a tendency to latch on, thinking how great they are for just treating you as a person.

He too was couch surfing as his mother had kicked him out. He was not a good person, and I remember him being very angry all the time. He was punk rock and drank heavily. One day we went to his mother's place to eat and shower while she was at work. I was starving and dirty, we both were. I can't remember if he lied to me about not being allowed there or not but she found out and called the police. I was arrested with him for breaking and entering and trespassing. This was the beginning of me becoming a ward of the court, which put me in and out of group homes and juvey.

When my dad found out I was arrested he came to see me and scared the shit out of me. He was so pissed about his truck being stolen and then repossessed. He always terrified me but at least I was safe in juvey and all he could do was talk to me. His one question was "Why, Julie? Why did you steal my truck while I was in jail?" My response was "I was scared of you. I thought you would kill me if I got caught and I couldn't come home. I hated it there and hated my life. For my protection I guess." I told the system of his drug dealing, and abuse which is what kept me in the system my whole teen life.

I was in three juvenile halls from the Inland Empire to Los Angeles. Some scarier than others. I was probably in five or more group homes over my teen years, always running and wanting to be free. It was hard to keep track because PTS clouded my mind, I was ALWAYS in fight or flight mode.

I lived on the streets from age fourteen to eighteen, in and out of group homes, juvey and back to the streets. Every time I was placed, I hated it and would run. This was a consistent pattern that would later repeat itself with my relationships and children.

The first group home I can remember going to caused one of the biggest scars I carried for many years. It was run by a Catholic Church, and located in Hemet, Ca. I met a girl there and we bonded immediately. We clicked and rebelled as a team. This is where Rebel Julie was born. She was needed for survival. No one cared for me, I hated the world and was a lost, scared little girl. So, I built my actions around the rebel archetype and used it when I needed to run. One night my new rebellious partner and I ran, planning to hitchhike back to Los Angeles. What was it about L.A.? I always ran there. We left late one moonless pitch-black night full of cloaking shadows. We had no idea what horrors awaited us in those shadows. We ran to the main highway, which was farther than expected, we were exhausted when a van pulled over and picked us up. We were so happy to be on our way to the freedom of LA. Little did we know the terror waiting for us in that van. This became one of the darkest and scariest moments in my life. After driving for a while, the driver pulled over on an off ramp in Riverside, about halfway to our goal of glamorous Los Angeles. That's when the hours of terror began. The driver raped us over and over again in that van.

It was beyond anything I had ever experienced; assault, pain, fear and disbelief became our world. Praying to my mom asking her to save us didn't stop the attacks. After hours of him repeating his acts of violence on us, suddenly we were released, thank God. I was so grateful that Mom had finally heard my pleas and intervened. We ran and ran to the nearest business. The rest of that night is a blur with parts etched in my memory. We suffered more humiliation when the cops came and took us to the hospital. Cut off from the only friend I knew at that moment; in separate areas with curtains drawn that offered the tiniest bit of security and safety, trying not to relive the terror but needing to answer questions in between sobs, I rolled into as small a ball as I could get, hugging my shaking abused body with my arms. With clenched fists and weak shaky one or two word replies to questions; I underwent the collection of a rape kit while feeling on display to all eyes even with that little curtain closed. Finally, we were taken back to the horrible group home, relieved to be back in a less unsafe place than we had been. I often wonder why it's called a group "home"; it is nothing like a HOME. There was never caring and compassion or safety for those of us who lived in those buildings.

\*\*\*

What I am about to tell you right now shocked me, scarred me and would end up being the reason behind my hatred of the church.

I remember laying in my bed, in shock, scared, hurting and alone in a state of numbness wondering how I didn't die, and what the fuck else was going to happen to me before the age of eighteen. A nun came to my bedside to console me. The only thing I remember from her words is this sentence that rings deeply in my soul to this day. "I am so sorry for what happened to you dear Julie. Let us pray together." Probably through my informational chart that followed me around, she had found out about my mom's suicide. When I told her how I prayed to her to help me survive my ordeal, she said words I will never forget; "well, I am sorry honey, but I want you to know your mom is not in heaven. She committed suicide and God does not allow people who commit this sin into heaven, she could not have helped you. It was GOD that helped you, not your mom." That created anger and rage deep within me, and in that moment, I cried and cried and cried, making a promise to myself to find out the truth behind what she just told me. This would be the reason behind my spiritual seeking and never settling with what the bible or church said to me. I knew what she said was not true but telling this to a fourteen-year-old girl who had just been repeatedly raped and subjected to many other horrors would change the lost little girl to a lost angry rebellious teenager on a mission to seek out the truth.

Not only did this ordeal wound me deeply, but while trying to understand it all I was scared to death because of my father again. He came to visit me while drugged out of his mind telling me, promising me, he would find my rapist and kill him. I was so scared on many levels: dad was a shell of a man, because of all the drug use, and it was devasting to see him like that. If he happened to find my rapist, I believed he would actually kill him, what would happen then? It was a scary moment seeing him like this. Looking back, I understand that he was feeling extreme guilt for the way he had treated me and this promise was a way for him to relieve himself of some responsibility. In reality, it was abundantly unlikely he would find the man, but my mind wasn't able to reason at that point. Feelings of fear and anguish washed over me.

The next four years were full of drugs, running, living on the streets, back to a group home, to juvey, to group home, running again and repeating the same; looking for someone or something to love and save me. I was so alone but determined to survive. Desperately searching for some sort of connection, I had many one-night stand lovers to help ease my pain. As a teenager seeking love, I just wanted to be cared for, to feel love, to feel secure. My body was what I had, and I used it to connect to whomever showed interest so I would feel desired, even for the short time we were together. I slept with many men just trying to feel something. After the rape, I boxed the event and my emotions tied to it, sealed it up all nice and tidy and put the box on the top shelf of my mind, making sure it was unable to come down and affect me. I had to live. I had to survive and nothing or no one was going to stop me. I didn't have time for feelings, at least feelings that anyone could see. I had a persona to uphold and had lots of experience hiding in plain sight. I was a tough, rebel punk rock girl who was hard and didn't need anyone. When underneath it all I was Lost Little Julie looking, longing for someone to love me. Where were they?

I was abandoned and totally alone but never once did I let that thought take form in my mind. I felt it deep inside, but didn't consciously acknowledge the idea at the time, if I pondered it too long it would kill me. I have to say sleeping on the streets, running, juvey and all the other things I experienced as a teenager is what I learned about growing up, becoming an adult, responsibility, and how to be loved. Which when I think about it, there was no love, there was no one. Just me, alone and surviving while occasionally lying with someone else. Later in life, the street training definitely played into and hindered so much when it came to being a mother. I never ever wanted any of my children to experience the life I lived, but there was really no choice; until I finally, years later, realized and understood I needed professional help. When looking at it now, it's not surprising how lack of guidance molded the rest of my life and my children's lives. I was too young to be a mother, even under the best circumstances. When I became pregnant, I wanted them so desperately because I wanted someone to love me unconditionally, I never understood the responsibility and the meaning of the word parent, mother or even father.

At age eighteen I left my last group home with a boy I met there. We ran to his dad's and did a lot of cocaine. He became abusive to me; thank God that was a very short time of my life. The days and nights here were full of anxiety, fear and once again being alone. What was I going to do now? I was eighteen with nowhere to go once again.

Soon I found myself back at Dad's place. I was just in time to see him leaving the state because he was sought by the cops for dealing. He was mentally gone and didn't even recognize me. When I went up to him in the local bar and said hello, he actually tried to grab my ass and hit on me. He didn't even recognize his own daughter. It had been three years since I had seen him, and all the drugs had taken the best of him. We had now changed places, I was ready to stop running and was hoping for, looking for, a safe place to grow into stability of some sort, not even sure what that looked like. He had lost everything, forgotten his daughter and was running away to his grandmas in Oregon. I felt he thought of me as just another mistake, a bad part of his life, and was shedding everything for a clean start. It didn't matter that at one time he considered me his daughter. I still feel the sadness of that day, watching him prepare to leave, disbelief washed over me like a wave. Disbelief that he was once a strong scary man I called Dad and now was a shell of a man lost in his own search for happiness. I know he blamed himself for my mom's death, which I felt he should, but it was heartbreaking to see my father that way.

**I** ended up going to live with my grandma, who had been my rock during my juvey and group home days. She would come to see me, try her best to help me and was the only one there for me.

I deeply love and appreciate Grandma for having hidden strength for both of us when needed most. She saved my life, guiding me as best she could, considering I was in deep rebellion. I have so much gratitude for her selfless nature and dedication to trying her best to make me feel loved and supported during that horrible time. I know it killed her a little bit everyday with thoughts of her own daughters' self-inflicted deaths, and thinking I might be next to follow suit in the suicide pact that ran so deep in our family. Her strength was something to admire. I didn't have the awareness then but now I often wonder how much agony was actually going on in her inner world.

At eighteen I arrived at Grandma's door pregnant. It was a lot to ask her to deal with. As always, she was there for me. The father was the boy I left the group home with. Obviously not a good pairing to bring up a baby. As a Christian, Grandma was not in support of abortion. With the common sense she had, she knew what the best option was, and she helped me to abort the pregnancy. I appreciate her so much for this because even though she knew it was against her beliefs she was rational enough to do what was best for me and the future of that baby.

While living with her, I got my first car, first job and first taste of normalcy in my life. Grandma's strength was astounding. She had been through her own hells in life, and I feel bad for the worries I caused her. When we are young, we don't take into consideration how our actions affect those closest to us, at least I didn't. I've come to understand it's part of childhood; to not realize or even consider older people were once young, lost and unsure; that they went through their own trauma. Grandma displayed wisdom and peace, seeming to have had the answers all her life. She had been through pain and suffering, endured through her own suffering, learning life so that she could help others, especially me. It never occurred to me that I might ask "how can I make it easier for you," instead of always taking from the very heart that was aching for me.

At nineteen, I met my first husband. He was twenty-seven, confident, stable and seemed to have life figured out. I had no idea what love looked like, I only knew what I saw growing up and that was the complete opposite of what I saw in him. Knowing what I had learned up to now was not even close to love, seeing him doing and saying things differently said to me "this must be love." I thought a normal life meant marriage, a child and happily ever after. Right? Isn't that every girl's dream? Well, it was mine at this age and time in my life. I just wanted safety, security and to be loved. I thought if I tried hard enough to love this man, I would be happy. We started dating, then moved in together, then I became pregnant. There was this intense desire within to be pregnant. I thought if I had a baby with someone it meant we were together forever, and I would be happy. For a time, it seemed as though all my prayers were answered.

On the outside our life looked perfect. We went to church as a family, we worked together, we had a baby. And I was miserable and exhausted from holding a wide personal space barrier so no one would get too close either physically or emotionally. This was not his fault, not either of our fault really. Love wasn't part of who I was at that time, I didn't know how to love, I was just going through motions that seemed to look like love. Who was I kidding? Myself mostly. It soon became apparent to others; guilt manifested as more self-hatred, heaped onto the shit pile of my life. Self-worth wasn't even in my vocabulary, not in my realm of life. Self-loathing was very real to me though. I felt guilty to have what I had always wanted, a home, husband and baby and still not feel worthy and happy. The guilt and deep insecurity overtook the ability to heal and flourish. There was no way I could discuss all these emotions with anyone, I was too guarded.

Looking back, my self-loathing was probably apparent because of my body language of stooped inward curved shoulders, self-isolation, inability to make eye contact or have a real conversation, along with many more outward clues, that I was an empty shell trying to just get through each day. I lacked so much and as time went on, I dragged a few souls along for this miserable ride with me, leaving brokenness in my wake. I feel true sorrow towards these souls; they know who they are.

When my son was eighteen months old, I finally decided to leave my husband and move on. I took my son with me for a few weeks, but after realizing motherhood was about responsibility and that was definitely something I lacked, I took him back to his father and left, alone again. Sadly, the time missed with him can never be reclaimed. It is something I will always regret but I have healed this part of my soul. We have healed together. I was twenty-one years old, and the rebellious party girl was bored with married life and being a mother. I ran from my feelings again; the pattern was deep. As hard as it is for me to say this, I had no idea how to be a mother, a wife, or anything other than a survivor. I went back to what I knew, what felt normal: chaos, drugs and running wild. Suddenly the cycle of my life was repeating, I was just a little older now.

Without a husband or baby to tie me down, I was out living what I thought was my best life; clubbing every night, sleeping around, losing myself even more, knowing the only thing that helped me feel better was seeking and finding something that temporarily felt good, made me feel special, and had no rules or responsibility. The next two years were all about one-night stands, looking for love in all the wrong places, and not seeing my son.

Not surprising, considering the life I led then, I became pregnant again. And guess what? I ran, as I always did when I wasn't comfortable with my circumstances. I figured the best way to make my life better was to ignore what I didn't like at that moment. So, I went to a lot of raves, partied all night, trying to escape the truth I was pregnant. I thought if I didn't feel her, I wouldn't make a connection, she wasn't real. At least that is what I told myself, and the more drugs I did the better I felt. Out of sight out of mind. As much as it hurts to tell the world my entire story; this book is about facing truths, acceptance and forgiveness. My rawness is needed so that we may all move into release, recovery and healing.

Grandma helped me get into drug rehab when I was about five months pregnant. It was scary and reminded me of the group homes I so hated growing up in. I met a boy there that I would later run away with one dark night.

The amazing parents of a girl I met in rehab took me in and allowed me to live there for about two months.

That was a brief and very much appreciated look into how kindness works. I not only continued to date the boy I left rehab with, but I also continued doing drugs and finding other men to sleep with. It is surprising how many men will sleep with a pregnant girl. I went to raves a lot, trying to ignore the little miracle inside me, staying as high as I could to make it through each day.

Grandma was influential in me showing some common sense, or was it Divine guidance, to seek out an adoption attorney.

I knew in my heart I could not give a baby the life she deserved, I decided to give my beautiful daughter up for adoption, knowing the only way she had a chance to grow and thrive was for someone else to take care of her.

Meeting with the attorney I looked through a photo album of potential parents. I saw them. Something in me just knew these were going to be her parents and give her the life I couldn't, give her the life I had dreamt of. This is what she deserved. Happiness, love and support. All the things I could not give her in the condition I was in.

I was open and honest with them about my drug use. They still accepted me, and their soon to be beautiful daughter. They treated me with kindness, helping me get an apartment, bought me decent clothes so I could look for a job, and continually gave me emotional support. I am forever grateful to them for treating me with love and for loving the little baby girl I later turned over to them. For the last months of my pregnancy, I felt supported, and loved. Not judged. I knew in my heart my daughter would be where she was always meant to be.

My baby daughter entered this world on a beautiful spring day. Only through Divine intervention, healing what I was unconsciously destroying, was she born healthy and beautiful. Through the haze of drugs one thing I knew for sure was I had no skills to take care of a baby at that time and thankfully I had found people who would be good parents for her.

Although I didn't know or understand at the time, my Guides had led me to her amazing and loving parents. I am beyond grateful for them. They loved and raised her, giving her a healthy life in all ways. Thank you for doing what I could not. She has grown to be smart, kind, compassionate and the best part of me. The truest part of me. The part I always wanted to be but never had the chance growing up. Giving her up was tough but I believe it was the right and best decision.

This scar went into another box, very high on the shelf of my mind and emotions. It had to be out of sight and out of mind so I could continue to stay alive. The wall was getting bigger and thicker. Could anyone ever save me? My lifelong desire had been to feel loved by someone, seen by someone. I felt having a child of my own would bring those things. Handing my daughter over to someone else was a loss I don't think I fully realized until much later in my life.

***

I did see my son off and on at my grandma's on weekends. I would have liked to see him more often but at the time I was giving all I had just to keep going day after day. Still using and mentally, emotionally and physically ill; most of the time I visited I was tripping or too tired to actually be present. Regret surrounding the whole situation chipped away at my soul causing extreme shame, guilt and grief. The combo of this and releasing my daughter in this turbulent three-year period caused a huge ugly wound that would seep out in many different ways through anger and fits of rage. Spiraling deeper, becoming more numb by drinking, and using more each day was how I chose to not think about everything I had done and been through.

After my daughter was born, I ended up back on the streets, with no place to call home.

Living from drug house to drug house, out of my car, and spiraling deeper into a dark and depressed state, my grandma once again came to my rescue. With help from her, I would soon have a place to live, and a new town to call home. I had an old friend I met when I was married to my first husband, and she lived in San Diego now. I moved to SD that year, in the summer after my daughter was born. It was an escape from this city, where all I knew was drugs, and fear. Once moved I stopped using and cleaned up my act.

While searching for work, which wasn't easy, I applied at a local topless bar. My roommate and I got jobs there and we were beyond excited but nervous of course. I mean after all dancing was my everything. And if I could get paid now to dance, and its only topless, why not? I was hooked.

I can tell you this experience only added more shame and pain to my soul, chipping away at my self-worth. The disgust in the men and how they choose who they tipped and who they didn't was what could be openly seen in that bar. There was also a dark underworld I wasn't familiar with. What goes on behind the scenes in those places are things only a few know. I only lasted for about two months, maybe less. It was too much for me. My friend/roommate and I had been fighting a lot during this time, and I couldn't be in the apartment anymore. I knew in my heart it was time to leave once again, the story of my life.

I had met a couple of brothers while living in San Diego. They would take me on a wild ride of psychedelics. Finding myself engulfed in the world of escape through these magical drugs, I really enjoyed experimenting with them. Going to my first Grateful Dead show was an experience in itself. I felt free and alive for the first time without a care in the world, learning a lot about myself, my body and how to love myself just a little bit.

One night with these two would end up being my last night in San Diego after going to a rave in the Mojave Desert hundreds of miles away.

That fateful night in the desert I would meet someone from my past, who would change the trajectory of my life one more time. Divine guidance would bring me through again.

That night the rave was everything you might imagine it would be: music, drugs, carnival rides, it had everything. After taking acid, I was high as one could be. By fated chance I saw an old friend of a friend. We connected and ended up leaving together with strangers because the brothers were nowhere to be found. So weird when I think about this, but then I realize Divine was steering me to my path still.

As we left the sun was rising, everyone was trying to find their cars, their rides, the rave was being taken down and me and my new (old) friend were alone.

The acquaintance I had found again and was hanging out with all night made friends with a couple of guys who ended up being our ride out of there. All I remember is sitting in the back seat praying to anyone who would listen that we would make it in one piece. This stranger, I am sure still tripping from the night of drugs, was driving over 100 miles an hour through the Angeles National Forest. I was also tripping and scared out of my mind. I just didn't want to die, not this way. How would my grandma find me? No one I was with knew who I was, much less where I lived or how to contact grandma, the only one who would care what happened to me.

Well, we made it to LA, thank God, and stayed with the guy my friend hooked up with. This lasted three days. When we left, she took me back to her house. Her parents took me in and loved me the best way they could. For the next six months or so they provided a place for me to live. Again, my method of operation was spending my time clubbing, partying, and being as checked out as possible. The only thing

I wanted to do was get high, probably because I was running from the pain of giving my daughter up and not having a father who gave a shit.

Meth once again became my best friend. The familiar cycle returned as being awake and up for days and days then sleeping for days and days, worrying her mother to death, wondering if I was okay or not. I owe so much gratitude to my friend and her family for at least keeping me as safe as they could, giving me food, and a place to lay my head at night.

Unfortunately, I was consistent in being consumed with myself only, my pain and my fucked-up world which led me to meet more strangers, more drug dealers, and a new house I called home. A drug house. Again? How did I get here?

It is all a fog of course. In the midst of all this shit, I would from time to time see my son. When I could pull myself together that is and give him a few hours of my precious drug seeking and using life. If I was lucky, I could stay at my grandma's and have a moment of peace.

There are many more stories to take you deeper into my life at this time, but what for? It was all the same, day after day, night after night. Repeated cycles of pain; continuing to feel lost and treating myself terribly because I felt I needed to punish myself for my daughter. I was not worthy of love; not from myself or anyone else. This is why I continued seeking out so many different souls in this same drugged fueled life. I was looking for someone to care, to save me and pick me up out of the muck. I didn't realize I wouldn't find help of any kind from those in their own shit hole. Like attracts like, right?

One day at my absolute bottom, I made the call from a drug house that saved my life. I reached out to the only person I could think of. Crying out for help, needing a place to go, a change, I called my brother. He opened his arms and home. At five feet, seven inches and one hundred pounds, I looked like a lost little girl shrunken by life, and that's who I was, scared, with nothing, a literal mess, I moved into his place in Los Angeles.

My brother is amazing, caring and loving. He cleaned me up physically, dressed me in new clothes and made me feel important. Sober for the first time in years I got a job and made friends. Finally, I felt safe and was living happily for a while, it was a good time for me.

Then I had another abortion. Trigger the dysfunction all over again.

Guilt and shame returned, and the learned avoidance tactics came back. After eighteen months of being clean and sober, I fell, started hanging out with the wrong crowd, staying out all night, doing drugs, lost my job and I left my brother's. The lost little girl showed up again, with additional shame and guilt. I believe she kept reappearing because I never really understood her. She would try to clean up, but always kept repeating the dysfunctional patterns, relying on what she knew, the comfort of drugs, avoidance and dissociation. I ended up living in an hourly rate motel, with the lowest of the low, working at the front desk for room and board. It was absolute darkness. In my stupor I had my grandma bring my son for a visit here. I don't know what I was thinking; obviously I wasn't thinking clearly. This only lasted a month or so, then I was on the streets again. The good thing is I had a car, but was back to zero, calling my grandma in desperate need of rescue. She picked me up, put me in rehab again where I stayed a month before going to live with her. She set rules and I listened, doing whatever she asked, so I could feel safe and at home; clean, happy and ready to start again.

iving with grandma I found a job at a local golf course as a waitress and bar tender. Most of my jobs throughout my life were the same. I was good looking and knew how to put the charm on to get good tips, knowing how to play the men. This was something I picked up early in my teens. I was a survivor, right? I needed to be manipulative so I could survive. A curse and a blessing I would say. My looks definitely helped along the way, but it also was my downfall once I realized how I could use not only my looks but my sex to control a situation. I never was a prostitute, but I did use sex to hopefully trap a casual partner into loving me. See, I thought sex was love because that is all I had ever been exposed to or taught. It would take me until my late forties to understand this, start to change my thoughts, release the programming and heal.

While working at the golf course I met my middle son's dad. He was also a bartender and a golfer. He came from generational wealth and had a life I was very attracted to which equaled stability in my mind; something I'd been looking for all my life. He was cute too! We flirted a lot and finally went out. We dated a while and I fell in love with him, at least the version of love I knew. Of course, at that time it was a physical attraction, not real love; I didn't know what that was.

My new partner's dad didn't like me and tried everything possible to get me out of the picture. He tried paying me off in many different ways, but I was in love and stuck it out. We got married became pregnant and soon my new husband enlisted in the

Army, leaving me alone again. Floundering and left to my own devices the only thing I knew to do was go back to my comfort zone of unhealthy behaviors. That song "Looking for love in all the wrong places" was my life. Lost Little Julie needed to feel wanted and numb the returning pain of abandonment. Thinking actions through and considering consequences was unheard of for me. What I did know about was Instant gratification and quick release of pain, so I reached out to an Ex to find it. It was never my intent to hurt people but that's what happened. Lacking personal development and not understanding the consequences of actions, I made all the wrong choices. So far, all the consequences of my actions were just put aside, ignored and self-medicated away. I did a lot of stuff without thinking it through.

I've come to realize being given drugs at such an early age, and never learning how to act responsibly left me in an emotional, physical and spiritual desert. Nothing was planted inside me, there was no life-giving water sprinkled on me. Life was about feeling good and surviving by any means. Being alone after my husband left for the Army put me in a vulnerable spot of wanting to feel loved and needing to sooth the neglected, rejected and forsaken wounds that kept being reopened and cut increasingly deeper.

Back then I had no idea of this shadow side of myself. I didn't even know the concept of that. Shadows were only places you avoided to stay safe, there was rarely anything good there. The notion of the ability to identify internal dark areas and work to shed light on them and therefore heal, was never

54

presented to me. Looking back, I see how those shadows were instrumental in bringing me to who and where I am today. I can now be thankful for them and better understand why I did the things I did. It was all because of patterns repeated from my early childhood of abandonment, neglect and loss.

After my husband went into the Army, by calling on my Ex and going back to the self-soothing things that made me feel better, I unknowingly set myself up for yet another failure. The relationship with my husband ended badly and it was all my fault. Living a life alone at home, surviving emotionally in the only way I knew how, was such a horrible thing to do to him, and something I never did again. Partying, sleeping around, being the only person I knew how to be hurt him deeply and hurt many others who crossed my path. I never deliberately caused grief or tormented anyone, but my actions did just that over and over again; until I learned how to deal with my own pain and trauma. I have worked through this part of myself, and I am here so that I can share how embracing and working with those shadows within led to understanding, and forgiveness, releasing me to be the Divine person I am meant to be, finding my true self.

My short marriage was annulled, and I moved in with the same Ex. This only lasted a few months because of more emotional mistreatment. Through Grace I only endured additional damage for a brief time. Soon I was back with Grandma about to have my middle son. He was born while living with her and she set rules again, thankfully. I had to go to AA meetings, get my GED, wake up early, contribute to the household and be responsible. It was the first time I had been shown how a responsible adult went through their days. Let me tell you it really helped me! That lady knew how to love while being tough because she was in Al-Anon for many years due to my grandpa being an alcoholic. She was the strongest and bravest woman I have known and I love Grandma deeply.

While I was living at grandma's my dad was also getting his shit together. A year or so before this he had gotten clean and decided to move back to the area where he and I used to live so he could be close to his brother. He enrolled in truck driving school and completely changed his life around. He was sober, got his own apartment and was doing great. He asked me if I wanted to move in with him and our healing journey began. Slowly, but it started. My son was a year old when we moved in. It was a good arrangement, as dad was driving for weeks at a time, and my son and I enjoyed the apartment and the time together. I didn't work, I was on welfare and just loved being a mom. I lived in the same complex as my first husband and oldest son, so I got to see him every day too. It was the first time I had both boys, I was clean and felt happy. At this time, I was also trying to make amends with my second husband for what took place last year.

He was still in the Army stationed in Georgia and we tried to work things out and possibly get back together, but our connection just wasn't there anymore. I took a trip to Georgia with his mom, and we did try to make it work but it just wasn't in the stars for us. My son and I lived with my dad for the next year or so. I had a best friend who lived in the desert, and we spent a lot of time together. She was my rock since I met her at age nineteen but with me always moving and not being stable, our friendship was always up and down. She was in a relationship with my first husband's brother and had two kids with him; they are cousins to my first son. We remained best friends for many years.

Eventually, I moved to the desert in my own place. I had been doing amazingly well, my dad and grandma helped me get a car, and for the first time I felt good as a functioning adult. I was learning how to be responsible for myself and my son. Life was feeling better each day, and I was excited to be an active participant in it, while blossoming into motherhood. I got a job and my own apartment. We were doing great. A sad bit of that blissful time was when my first son moved to Arizona with his dad, and our visits stopped. We didn't see each other for a while.

My second son's dad had been discharged and moved back to the area, taking our son for the weekend twice a month. During those weekends I really had fun with good friends I had made from work at another golf course close to home. We had a lot of get togethers, BBQs, dinners with my best friend and our kids and clubbing of course. My middle son got to spend a lot of time with his cousins. My life was feeling somewhat normal. Going through the motions of having a work group to hang with while including our families, was as close to an orderly life as I had ever been. I started drinking again because having fun meant drinking, right? I was thriving in my own single mom life and for the first time I felt like a regular responsible adult.

Even at this point I sometimes felt like I was fourteen. That teenager had not had the opportunity to grow and learn the progression into adulthood and at times she would come out full force doing the rebellious things teenagers do—like drinking, being sexually active and irresponsible. I thought I had it all together and was living a good life. At the time I didn't understand that those superficial activities don't make a healthy adult raising healthy children.

For the next couple of years, my son and I flourished while I worked. We simply lived, grew and enjoyed each other in the moment.

I started a relationship with someone who worked with me at the golf course. It was fun and at that time I considered it a typical romance. The problem was I had no idea what typical was. Learning to survive through manipulation I had found ways to control men and get what I wanted. This guy was much younger than me. At the time I figured I liked them young because I was young at heart, and I could control them with sex. He being younger than me was a good match, for a while. I felt admired by him because he was infatuated with me—more like infatuated with sex. Not knowing the difference between sex and love, I figured out how to control him; make sure he didn't leave; with sex. I thought he would one day fall in love with me. Thus, perpetuating my limited understanding that I could trade sex for love.

This attachment was off and on, and sometimes rocky. There was no substance, no real love, jut sex and fun. He was a good person, just young and not looking for more than I was able to give at that time. I grew a lot during this time, learning to make friends, live on my own and be a somewhat accountable adult. Thankfully I didn't get into much trouble, kept my job, and loved feeling normal, and being a mom. It was a good couple of years. But as had been my past cycles, that normalcy didn't last long.

I t was time to meet my youngest son's dad. The one who challenged me at my core. The one who ripped out my soul, helping me understand what I didn't want in a relationship.

We had an instant connection. Drawn together at first because we drank the same, later finding we partied and did drugs the same. We were too much alike to be a healthy relationship. Our dysfunctional families were very similar, his upbringing like mine; living with toxic parents who taught us about drugs early molded us to fit nicely together. It's easy to bond with someone who truly gets you in this way.

When we met and started dating, he was nineteen, I was ten years older physically but not emotionally or mentally. Feeling like a kid myself, it was fun to be with him because we were so much alike. If I had been more aware of this particular cycle of being drawn to a much younger man who didn't yet know how to treat someone he loved; I might have realized that we were doomed from the beginning. Between then and now I have often thought I could have saved myself from this particular heartache if I had been able to evaluate my ongoing life actions better. More recently, healing was initiated when I began to acknowledge this was another soul contract that happened exactly as it was meant to be, even though the lessons were rough and came with a high price.

We were in a relationship for six years, the longest bond (other than my grandma) I experienced in my life at that point. He is the father of my youngest son, and I profoundly believe we were destined to meet and have a child. After our son was born, we took a deep dive into drugs and partying.

Our connection was so strong that I felt like my life depended on being with him. I tried and tried to make him love me the way I knew I deserved but he didn't know how due to his own upbringing and abandonment issues. I didn't see this then, but I definitely see it now.

Our bond was strong because of the way we grew up; we had lived through the same type of childhood that few can relate to. I had come to depend on him as a form of safety, or at least how I viewed safety at the time. The relationship was toxic but for me that was nothing new and I had figured out a way to live in that.

I knew a relationship could be better, but I didn't know how to find or make that kind of connection.

My life pattern cycled through again and soon the self-sabotage started back up. Using meth and clubbing almost every day was the structure I returned to. This was typical for my life at that time. When things began to look normal, I always found a way to undermine progress.

Even with the drug use I was making a good home for my son and the new baby. My two boys and I were living what felt like a perfect little life.

Suddenly out of the blue my ex-husband and his wife took me to court for full custody of my seven-year-old (middle) son. They believed my drug use was putting him in danger. I admit I was using drugs at the time, but I was holding down a job, keeping an apartment and was making a good home for our little family. I was blindsided, completely flabbergasted and felt like my soul had been ripped from my chest. I was adamant to fight them and not allow my son to be taken from me. We weren't allowed to see each other for two months during the custody suit and it was an extremely difficult time. I had worked hard to make what I thought was a good life for us. Now I was facing the real possibility of losing him forever.

Grandma blessed us by hiring an attorney to fight this battle. Mediation was scheduled and I was scared to death. On the appearance day neither my ex nor his wife showed up. That seeming lack of interest on their part was why my son and I were instantly reunited. With a head buzzing in excitement and anticipation, envisioning us home together and happy again, in my mind I lifted my boy up and was swinging him around. Suddenly the judge's next words hit me in the chest, taking my breath away. The ruling continued, declaring he was not allowed to live with me any longer. In one instant I felt blood draining from my face as I dropped into the darkness of despair and depression. It was a bittersweet day. We were reunited briefly and suddenly he was ripped out of my life, changing my whole world in an instant. The judge awarded his dad physical custody with me getting every other weekend visits. This changed my life forever and began my deep dive into the spiritual side of life.

At the time I couldn't see that my actions of *just* dabbling in drugs were causing any harm. I now see that I was walking on the edge poised to fall deeper at any moment. I wasn't well, I wasn't even okay. My head was above water only because, for my sons, I could function in society, keep a job and a place to live. There wasn't capacity to thrive and steer my son in an emotionally healthy way. That is probably what the judge saw and was protecting my son from. After the ruling and our separation, I started using more and more, depending on drugs to get up, work and function day to day. Lying to myself I thought "I don't stay up all night, and party, I just use a little more each day to keep going." I needed to numb myself because now I only saw my son every other weekend.

The wound was deep and the only way I knew how to work through was to not feel it. On our biweekly visits I saw this little boy who was once carefree and happy change into a different person. I think what his dad did changed something inside him. He would come to my house telling me horrible stories about his living situation while becoming angrier and more defiant. Seeing my boy decline and not being able to do anything about it dug deeper and deeper each time I saw him. I was bleeding on the inside feeling helpless and hopeless. Deep sadness brought up that old hollowness. What that meant in my life cycle was numbing my pain the only way I knew how which was drugs and alcohol at that time.

Grandma loved my son dearly and was devastated as well to see the toll life was taking on him. She knew deep in her soul I was struggling with drugs and drinking again, and this was weighing heavily on her. Unhealed life patterns show themselves under stress. Here I was again trying to survive and get through these current changes, upheavals and demands. Drugs were always a way for me to escape my feelings of being a lost unwanted soul. I had always wanted to be a part of a loving caring family and tried so hard to make it happen. That craving was replaced with drugs when my son was taken from me. The void and profound sense of loss took me back to that unsafe Little Girl who just wanted to have someone care for her as she cared for others in her family.

Breaking apart the home I had lovingly made not only shattered the family unit and my lifelong dreams, it also tore open those old wounds. Feelings of security and belonging vanished. Survival mode kicked in as I was trying to cope and navigate the pain. In came the reoccurring management mechanisms of running away emotionally and hiding from life. The standbys of drugs and alcohol allowed me to easily be in the space of disconnect. An addict is never cured, they simply use the tools they have come to know until they learn new tools. This had me embedded yet again in the repeating cycles my life went through.

All of this also added to the decline of the shaky, insubstantial relationship between me and the father of my youngest son. We were both using and getting deeper and deeper into our toxic dysfunctional cycles that we knew as the familiar patterns we were raised with. We moved further and further apart. He was abusive, I was abusive and together it was like pouring gasoline on a fire.

I had no idea something was about to shift in my life. Once you have a spiritual awakening there is no going back.

The person I was with at this time, whom I had been with the longest in my life so far was very willing and able to supply what I needed just then in terms of drugs, alcohol and a party partner.

Leaving this long-term relationship is one of the hardest things I've done. I felt we were made for each other, we had so much in common. We were using meth and choosing to live in darkness together. Even through the toxicity, I depended on him.

I believe deep in my soul that the breakup was orchestrated by my spiritual team, and no one can tell me otherwise. It was extremely difficult for me to leave, and I probably wouldn't have if Spirit hadn't stepped in. I was entrenched in the fox hole of my battles, and he was right there with me the whole time.

Through many whispers and synchronicities, what some call coincidences, I was led to finally disengage from the codependence. I call it being Divinely led or Whispers to my soul. The Light shined out of the blue one day in a chance meeting with the woman he was trying to have an affair with. The truth was literally staring me in the face. That became the catalyst to finally empower me to walk out that door and never go back. All the toxicity couldn't push me out of the situation that seemed so comfortable and right in many ways, but when I noticed signs and messages from Spirit that he was at least mentally cheating, there was no looking back. Betrayal was the only thing that could have pushed me to finally seek freedom. What I needed to do became perfectly clear and aligned as Spirit led me in the steps to separate from that relationship which was poisonous to my body and soul. I was running out of time, literally dying a slow death.

Even though leaving was the best for me, I will always love and care about him. He held my broken heart for a long time. Unfortunately, his life has become even more toxic and destructive, and I am honestly glad I made the most difficult decision to leave him. This act was the beginning of my first spiritual awakening, and the veil would be lifted for me to peek through at another way of living.

Up to this point in my life, I was a magnet for every type of drama imaginable. Playing the victim and carrying a ball and chain to my past made me bitter and full of anger. I was a shell of a human, not caring about anyone or anything other than myself, feeling sorry for myself and continuing to repeat patterns, falling short of my true worth.

The universe helped and guided me to make this separation happen so I could become whole. The backstory of being poisoned and getting closer and closer to dying in the flesh wasn't clear to me at the time; I've come to understand that now. I was destined to meet the angel who would help me start seeing the Light in my soul. It was necessary for me to clear that unhealthy attachment so there was room in my life for a new, healing connection.

I was about to discover so much about myself, my soul, with the upcoming first attempt to crack open my dark soul allowing a little light to shine through.

The magic of the Universe made itself very clear to me between this and the next year.

Four months after I left the person I thought was the love of my life, I met a man who would completely shift my belief in relationships, how I was supposed to be treated, and help me conquer the demon that was tied to my soul at that time. I like to call him a soul mate. The term soul mate here is about this person's soul touching mine as a guide, not necessarily in the romantic way it is often used. The Universe sent him to me to help me get off drugs and get through my grandma's death. He was a huge part of my spiritual awakening, and the reason behind the beginning of my healing journey. I had a deep love for him, and he for me. He showed me what love was really supposed to be from the beginning. How I should respectfully be treated, and be heard, cared for and safe.

*Part Two*

# The Root

*"Through trials, I've bloomed, through pain, I've found that love is the root where strength is bound.*

*Through bitter winds and shadowed skies, it holds the dream where hope still lies."*

got a taste of what I thought true love felt like. He was a man with a conscience plan, well mannered, safe, handsome, reliable, and he loved me. He helped me see what I deserved in love. He taught me to stand up for myself, my worth, and he loved me in spite of my flaws. One flaw I hid from him was the fact I was still using drugs daily to function, but I would sleep every night. I took uppers in the morning and throughout the day, and Xanax at night to sleep. I only ate donuts and Reese's peanut butter cups. Still in the habit of using and lying to everyone who knew me, including my current boyfriend, my soul mate who helped me through more than I think he even knew, I hid a certain part of myself that I couldn't shake no matter how much I wanted to.

I was skinny and barely hanging on. In this six-month period, I was also studying quite a bit of metaphysical material. I dove deep into kabbalah, tarot, numerology and astrology. The drugs helped me focus and I did learn a lot in this period, but I was a shell, a liar to this man, to everyone. The spiritual seed had been planted, and I knew at that moment I needed to change, truly change who I was. I owed it to him to tell the truth. I made a plan to stop in November and come clean to him. November 11, I stopped using speed and slept for a week straight. I vowed to eventually tell him the truth.

Once I was clean and felt somewhat normal, we had dinner together. I knew in that moment if I ever wanted a different path, and different way of living, I would need to tell him everything. He loved me so much and if I lost him, it was my own fault.

For the first time in my life, I came clean and told him everything. How I was using speed daily, in the bathroom, in restaurant bathrooms, everywhere, anywhere, all the time. I had never been so scared in my life. Exposed, knowing I was opening the closet door and vulnerable to be judged, to hurt him, to lay my heart on the line. But I did it because I knew he deserved the truth and if it was meant to be, he would understand and stay.

The truth blew him away of course. How embarrassing for him, not knowing what I was doing right under his nose. I think he was more hurt and embarrassed than mad. It took him a few weeks to come to the conclusion he loved me enough to work through it and we stayed together another year until I said goodbye to him.

The next month my life was completely turned upside down, when my grandma fell sick, never recovered and died on December 9, 2005. When she was hospitalized, she begged and pleaded with me to stop drinking and get clean.

My grandma was a tortured soul who put everyone above herself. She survived so much loss throughout her life, and I'm sure trying to be there for me was very difficult for her.

I never stopped to think how she was feeling or doing all those years before. She seemed so strong, so independent and eager to help. She practiced tough love with me; not allowing me to stay with her when I was at my worst but offering me a ride to the Salvation Army was a telltale sign of her strength. At that time, I was so angry with her because I thought she just didn't care but it was quite the opposite. She did care, and that was why she was doing it.

Grandma was very familiar with the 12-step program Al-Anon for family and friends of alcoholics. My grandpa was an alcoholic. She used her learned coping skills and tools with me not only during this time but later when she would allow me to move in and made a contract with me in order to live there. She was the one constant in my life, from my teens to adulthood. She was my biggest cheerleader so when she passed it completely devastated me. She lost both of her daughters to suicide and her husband died nine months before my mom, her second daughter to die by suicide. The pain of all that must have been enormous, but she never showed it.

Grandma was not only someone who survived extreme traumas, she became a pillar of strength wanting desperately to help others in spite of her own pain. She was intensely dedicated to the Christian faith, and was highly active in her church activities which I think was her strength. I am in awe of her and always have been.

She never really said drugs to my face, she blamed all my downfalls on alcohol. We argued while she was in the hospital and her one wish was, I would stop drinking and not end up like grandpa who died as a result of alcohol abuse. I saw how worried she was for me, and what she didn't know was I recently got clean from drugs, and my boyfriend and I were in an amazing place. So, I could easily assure her and promise I would be okay. At the end of our conversation, the color came back into her face and she was sitting up and laughing. We hugged and I thought she would recover. She looked so much happier and not worried about me anymore. Through her Christian faith and our heart-to-heart conversation, she had found forgiveness and peace in her heart and soul. Believing I would be safe and taken care of, knowing I would be okay, she was ready. Ready to go home. It was almost as if she already knew this would be her last day in this painful world.

That night she coded and two days later we lost her. Ironically, the hospital didn't get the DNR into her file. Therefore, they attempted to save her life by resuscitation and other interventions considered to be the best thing to do. This unfortunately caused two days of terror for her. With a tube down her throat keeping her in the painful world, I could see the fear in her eyes. She was not allowed to slip off into the other realm she believed was heaven in the peaceful way she had worked hard to achieve and that hurts my heart.

Her sister and my brother came to the hospital, and we all met with the doctors. We asked them why they didn't see the DNR? Why is she strapped to the bed, with a tube in her mouth? WHY? We were so angry. The fear she had in her eyes was all we needed to see. We decided to finally have them take out the tube and allow her to drift away peacefully.

And just like that her soul left in the most peaceful way possible. She was relieved and with her husband and two daughters. It was beautiful to see her at peace, but I was devastated. I was lost without her and was numb.

In her death, I learned when you are ready you are ready, and when she was at peace, I believe she was ready.

My boyfriend, my soulmate, was my rock and helped me to get over her death. My first spiritual awakening came just after Grandma's death. Over the next year, I thrived, healed, and really dug deep into my spiritual practice. I stopped drinking and wasn't using drugs anymore. Life was good at this time. I slowly stepped into my true self; my integrity, my values and my core changed. I started becoming very intuitive, speaking with spirit and seeking my soul's yearning every day. In my darkest moment after losing her, I started to find myself. It was as if she was helping me from the other side, gently guiding me and whispering to my soul as I started my new spiritual journey. I was finding myself, my calling.

About a year after Grandma died, my boyfriend and I moved in together. He took me out of the desert, literally. With him I was able to physically move from the desert, which he hated, and he watered and cared for the desert of my soul so I could begin to grow and blossom inside. We only lived together for a short time. Even though we both seemed to prosper in this new life, we soon began growing apart. I started to change, becoming insecure. Self-doubt crept in and uncertainty began chipping away at my mental health. I began gaining weight and chastised myself for that too. I felt him pulling away from me, and that caused me to withdraw from him internally then outwardly.

I had just gotten an amazing job in the medical field, making more money than I had before, and it was time to branch out on my own. I had a feeling he was looking elsewhere for love. Intuitively I felt our relationship was over, and there was nothing left to fight for. Learned patterns to protect myself is where I went. I started to sabotage our relationship. Even though I knew intuitively it was time to leave, I could have done it with more love and compassion. But remember, I was still a baby spiritually and emotionally and didn't know anything else to do other than run. Run. Run. Run.

I should have sat down and talked to him, but instead my reoccurring cycle of running from problems kicked in and I packed up the whole apartment and left while he was at work. He came home and everything was gone. Before he could hurt me, I hurt him. Less than a year later he had a baby, so my intuition was on point, which was great confirmation, but I could have tried a little harder to make the separation easier. Today I am still working through some guilt from how I handled this part of our time together, I do regret the pain I am sure I caused him, but I believed leaving that way was my only option. I look back now and know it was because our time together was done.

My Knowing tells me his mission was to help me through one of the hardest times in my life with grace and dignity. He was an angel, showed me unconditional love and support when I needed it the most. I will always have a special place in my heart for him. The way I left was very mean, it was the only way I knew to protect myself. Self-sabotaging patterns resurfaced as I talked myself into what I felt was best and running was the safe feeling I knew, what I had learned. With all the growth in the past few years, that part was still a basic instinct for me.

For the next five years I fought to become myself. To heal myself. To love myself and dig as deep as I could spiritually and learn as much as possible. I ended up in Redlands after leaving him, in my own apartment with my two boys. For the first time I felt like my life was really changing. I was on my own, had a great job and was handling everything financially myself. It felt good.

The pressures of being a single mom, wanting to drink and go out started taking over, once again. The job I was working at started being toxic and draining. So, I would drink more and more, going out more and more. Over the first year on my own, things started to fall apart, eventually I lost my job, and was going to lose my apartment. My dad had just bought a mobile home and somehow, I found myself living with him. I truly don't remember how it all happened, how I ended up with him again but there I was and there he was, willing to help me and my boys for the first time in my life, or his for that matter.

I lived with him for a year with no job, just being able to relax for the first time and allow my dad to help me. It felt good and safe. He was finally able to help me and my boys, and all I wanted to do was heal our relationship. I loved him so much and always looked up to him even through the fear and everything he did when I was growing up.

I remember him telling me that my grandma asked him to promise her that he would take care of me, no matter what. His words to me were "your grandma made me promise I would never leave you again and always take care of you. This is my promise to you and her." And he kept that promise until the day he died and even after his death, I feel he has had his hand in many of my successes.

I began working in the medical field again, still living with Dad along with my oldest and youngest boys. I vowed to always be there for my boys, especially the youngest. There was a point when he was five, I almost allowed him to move to his dad's, because I was falling into old patterns, but I came to my senses and stopped that quickly. During that time, I also vowed to remain single until I understood who I am, what I deserve, and not keep repeating patterns of dysfunctional relationships so my children didn't repeatedly see the same. I am still single to this day.

I was healing and I wanted to guide my children to heal also. There was so much brokenness to be looked at and learn how to live life better. We were starting the process of becoming whole again.

At the end of 2009, I learned about this amazing opportunity called surrogacy. In my clinic we had girls come through who were surrogates, and I thought wow, this is something I can do, and it would change my life. I could go back to school, work from home, and be there for my kids. I looked into it and became a surrogate twice, in 2011 and 2013.

It allowed me to be a stay-at-home mom and dedicate love to my children and myself. It was such a happy time in all of our lives. I started noticing all the whispers, the synchronicities in my life at this time. My faith was growing and everything started turning around. I felt safe, protected by my dad's love and I was a good mom to my boys. Normalcy started to be a thing of the present, not just something I used to dream of.

I enrolled in Sedona University for my bachelor's degree in Metaphysical Science. I knew I needed to deepen my spiritual practice, work on healing myself, and in turn help others. I studied New Thought teaching from the University and in doing so I really began to see my connection to Source, the healing I needed to do and what to let go of. I learned about forgiveness of self and others in order to be set free. I really dug deep inside myself over these two years. I like to say what I learned from Kabbalah, my tarot, speaking with my guides and building my faith genuinely started planting seeds that were starting to sprout.

Surrogacy taught me unconditional love and giving back and I do believe that facilitated tremendous healing in me as well.

During my first surrogacy I went to see a spiritual therapist and did a lot of past life regression work, and balancing of my chakras (the energy centers in my body). I also learned about my shadow self and started diving into these aspects of who I was. I received my bachelor's degree in metaphysical science, as well as becoming an ordained minister in 2012. My plan was to start seeing clients one on one and also start helping those stuck in the church to see the light within them rather than in a place, person or thing out there somewhere. I never started with that dream, but I did help my closest friends with their lives and situations. I was feeling fulfilled. I am now in a place of love for myself and others and it might be time for me to reignite that dream soon.

I still studied everything spiritual I could and kept soaking up knowledge as it came. I believe you can never stop unlearning and re-learning who you really are. What I know about my sacred self today was always inside me, and all the things I dabbled in, studied and learned illuminated what I already knew deep within my soul. I believe my surrogacy and what I gained at Sedona University were Divinely timed parts of a spiritual awakening and everything started making sense. The synchronicities happened every day, and as time went on, they grew more and more intense. My life started taking a nice turn and things were finally working out for me. Miracles really do happen.

Along with my inner self-work, I took classes to be an addiction counselor because I knew I wanted to help others in a WHOLEistic way. Addiction and unhealed trauma go hand in hand, so it was important for me to learn this integrated vocation. I did receive my certificate to be an addiction counselor, but that went on the shelf until years later.

I gave birth to my first surrogate baby in June 2011 and this time in my life was so wonderful and beautiful as I was living the life I was meant to.

Things were going great, my best friend was living with me, and my dad had retired and moved to Washington with his mother. Life was good.

I was pregnant with my second surrogate baby and on bedrest from week sixteen through week thirty-six. This was due to a shortened cervix and the possibility of miscarriage. My sister-in-law from my first marriage, who had become and stayed my best friend, was living with me and she was there to help me on a daily basis acting as a companion and caregiver. The surrogacy agency was able to pay for this kind of care and it was a godsend to both of us. I wasn't allowed to do much, which made me very dependent on her. We did have a good time; we were good for each other. I felt loved and taken care of during this time. Her care allowed me to stay healthy and keep the baby I was carrying safe. There was a lot of time to study more while resting as much as needed.

Just a month after the delivery, I received a call from dad while he was in the ER. He sounded horrible, and the news he was about to share took me outside of my body. Little did I know another major life altering event was about to happen that would turn my world upside down, literally.

We learned he had stage 4 lung cancer and only had maybe six months to live. After his call, I flew up to Washington and stayed a few weeks attending appointments with him. Together we heard the devastating news. Six months, what? I was shaky with a cold heaviness in the pit of my stomach. The man who was so strong and, in my mind, would live forever was going to die. Why? Teary eyed, I had so many questions. It was hard to breathe. The doctor's voice sounded far away. Feeling myself sway slightly I protectively crossed my arms in front of myself. I tried to form the questions, tried to process this news. We were in such a good place; he had retired and was happy. It couldn't be true, there must be a mistake. Knocked back down, with another life altering event that would forever change my once safe, boring and routine life, I soon was going to be thrust into a life-threatening space.

It wasn't a mistake. In August, he drove back down to California to die in his own home. We set him up with hospice and allowed him to spend his final days at home as he wished. We had long talks and I told him "Daddy, I forgive you. Please know mom does too, and I love you and only want you to pass peacefully." I could feel that he still carried a lot of guilt and shame about the part he played in Mom's suicide and the subsequent way he fathered us; unable to quiet his beasts within. I know he never consciously meant to hurt her or me and my brother. He was a product of his upbringing, as we all are to a degree, but he was never able to do better with and for us until we were both much older. He became my rock, being there for me and my sons before he got sick. The weekend of September 28, he took a turn for the worse. He blacked out, hit me and became someone I didn't know; I was terrified and alone with him. That day is the day I lost my dad. He went into a coma, and died on Oct 4, 2013, a shell of a man, a lost soul scarred by this world. His death was heartbreaking in many ways; dark, psychotic, wrestling with visions, full of fear. His judgment day was loud, far from peaceful. I believe his illness was manifested from all his resentment, guilt and fear, not able to forgive himself for what he did throughout his life. It was tragic to watch and not something I would ever want anyone to go through. When he passed, I had a minister friend come over and sage and clear the house, helping him pass over to the other side. I felt like he was stuck in between worlds, not being able to accept his life and his actions. I am not sure when he finally was able to find peace, but I know the following year my life took an unexpected turn for the better and I believe he had his hand in it. Today I know without a doubt he is at peace and caring for me the way he wanted to when he was on earth. I feel him guiding me and taking care of Little Julie in a big girl body. I learned so much from Dad's life and death. It would take another book to explain it all. With gratitude I am now able to say, "clean up your side of the street because this life is either your heaven or hell, your choice on how your life is lived and how you will die."

During the time I lived with my dad, I developed a neighbor friend who was 103 years old. We spent many nights together sharing stories and wine. He lived alone, having lost his wife many years prior. I hold close to my heart the time we spent together. He was such a genuine soul, happy, upbeat and the stories he would share will forever remain in my memory. It was such an innocent time with him, he held and shared so much joy.

Two weeks after my dad passed, we found my sweet neighbor dead in his room by a self-inflicted gunshot wound. I was shocked and horrified of the timing and another blow of pain and grief all hit me at once. I honestly think the death of my dad and the pain he saw in my eyes was too much for him to bear. He didn't know what to say to me, and with everything happening in my life I was spending less and less time with him. I sometimes wonder if I wasn't caught up in my own pain, and made more time for him that night may not of happened the way it did. Something I pondered, adding to my guilt. I started drinking heavily and dabbled back into speed. It was my go-to always making me feel better. Or more accurately, making me NOT feel the deep intense unmanageable pain. I fell back into familiar patterns I was so comfortable with knowing my pain and agony would be taken away even temporarily. This was such a learned habit from early childhood that it was the only way I knew how to silence and numb the misery creeping back in and becoming center stage in my life again. The shame of using, the guilt of it all and the continual patterns emerged once again. At the time I didn't fully understand that 'dabbling' with a substance opens the door wide for an addict.

Part way through that hellacious month of October I received a text from my daughter, whom I had put up for adoption. She told me her adoptive father had passed away from ALS at home on hospice. Coincidently, her father had died two days after my father. I was in shock, and my heart went out to her. She was feeling her first major loss, and painful tragedy that I was so familiar with. All I could think was *no, not her*. I wanted to protect her from these experiences, I wanted to protect all of my children from any of these life events, knowing in my head I really couldn't. I would have gladly taken this pain from her, but we know that isn't possible. I no longer believe in coincidences and know with all my being this Divinely timed connection was the reason we met a couple months later.

Even though our meeting was because of the great loss we shared, it was a blessing to see my daughter for the first time since I gave birth to her. What would I say to her? Would the shame and guilt of giving her up all those years ago get the best of me? My mind was spinning in fear.

Seeing and talking with the daughter I had given up brought back feelings of guilt for what I had done, even though I know the difficult choice I made for her might likely have saved her life. Just because it was the best decision doesn't mean it was easy or what my mother's heart wanted. Seeing her again tore open the loss and mourning wound. It felt like my heart was breaking again, like I was bleeding on the inside where no one could see, where the shame, regret and anxiety had been living quietly for all these years. Along with all that, I was full of gratitude and thankfulness she had been loved, kept healthy and raised in a stable home full of love. I wished I could change what had happened with my daughter, Dad and my neighbor friend. There was a constant tightness in my chest, and it was painful to even breathe. I can't remember all the feelings and emotions that were bubbling inside me at that time.

85

I do remember a heavy dark cloak of regret and overwhelm was what I was wearing. That cloak of despair, along with profound loss I felt for my Dad, my friend, seeing my daughter face to face reminded me of what I had missed with her and maybe more importantly, even loss of my new self now. I could feel the new growth, the accomplishments slipping away. That cloak squeezed me harder, and I couldn't breathe, couldn't cope. I felt the urge to run again. The layers of pain were getting more than I could bear and I was scared and out of control, knowing what was building within. Each hour that passed it became harder and harder to maintain any kind of stability.

Before October, even though I had been doing better physically, feeling like my life was becoming healthier in many ways, I hadn't yet learned how to process all the shadows within. The month from hell washed over me, took me under gulping for air, I had no lifeline. I started drinking to ease the pain, my days were filled with tears, drinking, grief, insomnia, physical pain and more drinking. The days turned into months with a new year looming. I couldn't see or feel hope for myself and my life. The pain inside and outside my body, in my mind and psyche was massive and uncontrollable. I don't think it was a coherent idea, but I decided to do what I had always done, run. RUN! RUN was my only real thought. I didn't know where to run though. Grandma was gone, Dad was gone, the friend I spent so much time with was gone. RUN! RUN! Kept screaming in my brain. I was like a trapped animal. Trapped within, unable to break free and think clearly. RUN! RUN! That had always helped before.

It all came crashing down on New Year's Eve when it seemed there was only one place to run and get away from the pain and mess of my life. In those voices and feelings, a thought formed of leaving this earth permanently. There didn't seem to be another option, I was so very tired of the rollercoaster ride that only gave relief from the screaming within for short sporadic times.

I attempted suicide by taking a handful of pills. My youngest found me, an ambulance was called, and I was taken to the hospital where my stomach was pumped, and I was placed on a 72-hour hold. My best friend called my other sons. While I was out, I felt like I went to another place and time and talked to my dad, grandma and mom. I woke up with a knowing something was different. The next three days were eye opening and a major turning point in my life. Locked away from the world, alone again, I read a book that changed my thinking. I started to see another way to live, other than allowing the victim to remain in the driver's seat. The book was "Life without Limits" by Nick Vujicic. It really started to change my perspective on life, and I was ready to start living again.

I felt fresh, ready for change and looked forward to taking a different path in my life. I am so grateful I was given the chance to stay, turn the corner and become who I am today. That was the turning point for change, and I would be blown away by what the universe was about to present to me. Remember faith is my superpower and over the years it has only gotten stronger and stronger.

\*\*\*

Here I want to apologize to my kids for my actions on New Year's day. What I did wasn't fair. It wasn't ok to put you in that situation. I am truly sorry, and please know I only wanted to go to sleep and make all the pain go away. I needed the pain to stop. I needed a break from the repeated cycles, the shame, the guilt and everything that was weighing me down at that time. I apologize for not considering your feelings in all this mess. I can't imagine what you must have felt watching me spiraling down, down, down while drinking more and more trying to numb away the pain. In that careless and selfish moment, I left a scar on your souls that I will forever regret.

\*\*\*

The rest of that year that started out so horribly became a time full of putting me first, going out and getting a job and feeling good with me. I was prescribed antidepressants and started to put what I had learned spiritually into play. I stopped drinking and focused on working. I found a job at a DUI program near my home, and it was good to just be out of the house. The pay was horrible, but it felt good to give back to the community and earn some money again. That job only lasted a little bit before I found another job as a medical assistant in an ortho office. This place would be another turning point for me and the reason I rose up and had the job opportunity of a lifetime fall into my lap. Healing between my brother and I had already started as we were getting close again after my dad died. I would go and stay with him at times, and he would take my boys and I on weekend trips to Palm Springs. We started celebrating our birthdays together with brother sister birthday weekends, becoming a yearly celebration that has lasted through today.

The next major change in my life would come straight out of the blue. Serendipity! One of my favorite words.

The intake coordinator from the surrogacy program I was previously involved in contacted me asking if I wanted to do home visits part time in the same type of program she was currently working with. This was so unexpected, and I was excited. I had remained in contact with her, and we had discussed the possibility of writing a book together. She knew my passion for helping families through surrogacy. We met for lunch while I was visiting my brother. Her proposal sounded like something I could do part time and make a little extra money, so I gladly said yes.

There were many reasons I wanted to take this very part time job, one of the main ones was I hated the job I was currently working. They took advantage of their employees and would move positions around without even asking us. They took my MA position away and offered me a new position as collections assistant. The offer came with a raise and promotion, but I was blown away with the way they handled the whole thing, and I knew hassling people to get them to pay a bill was not the job for me. I looked at them and said "I am sorry but no. I do not want this job, I quit." I don't know what came over me, I had no income except the part time home visits, but one thing I did have was faith. I knew if I walked out, the universe would take care of me. It always did, especially if it had to do with my integrity and going against something I didn't believe in.

Little did I know this day would change the direction of my life. I said "I quit", walked out and didn't look back. Was I emotional? Yes! Was I scared? Yes, but I knew the universe would take care of me. I had a coworker at the time who was a very close friend and loved my youngest son. When she saw me walk out, she came outside and had a real heart to heart with me. She could not comprehend how I could just walk out of a job, with no other job lined up or income to take care of my children. I remember telling her, "I will be fine, I just know it. What they did to me was unacceptable, and I won't be bullied into a position that isn't meant for me." We talked for a while. I was crying because I didn't understand how they could do this to me. I thought I was up for a promotion to the medical assisting side of the business. Then suddenly that job was pulled away from me, and I was lied to, not given a choice and offered the horrible position of collections representative. Management knew collections wasn't a good fit for me. That hurt as much as losing the seemingly perfect promotion. There was no way in hell I was going to stand for this. I guess you can say Rebel Julie was coming out, and at times she had my back in the best way possible.

On my drive home, I talked to the universe, my dad, grandma and mom asking for help. I talked to myself, self-soothing and internally defending my action. That car ride home was about to be the last time I needed to worry about money for a long time, but I didn't know it just then. I was about to get a phone call which was nothing short of a miracle, or Divine timing, whichever you believe in. I look at it as perfect timing while being held in the arms of Divine Mother as she rocked me cooing *'everything is going to be ok, Julie, trust me.'*

I got home and went directly to my best friend's house. I was talking and crying and hurting with her about everything that happened that day. I hadn't told anyone else what had happened; the discouragement while knowing I had done the right thing for me, keeping my integrity intact by leaving my job.

Two hours later, the call that changed my life came. The phone rang and the owner of the organization I was doing home visits for was on the line. He offered me a full-time job making more money than I ever thought was possible for me, even though I always knew I was worthy of more. It was the amount I had been continually thinking about at my previous job. The amount I was worth, the amount that would allow me to live a good life. The timing of this synchronicity still amazes me today. It was magical and I believe if I hadn't taken initiative and been brave enough to walk out of the job that was totally wrong for me, move that stifling, confining, heavy energy by walking out, the offer for the perfect position would not have fallen into my lap. Karmic connections were being revealed.

I took the job in Beverly Hills, as a surrogacy Intake Coordinator and Case Manager. This step led me down a path that forever changed me for the better. At this time, my middle son graduated high school and went straight into the army; something he had wanted to do since he was a little boy. His father was in the army, and I think it was important to him to follow suit and make a connection with his father in this way. I also think he wanted to escape our dysfunctional family and begin his own solo journey. It would be a few years before he came to LA for a visit. He was and is a very independent man.

For about eight months I commuted along the abrasive Southern California freeways before finding a house near the surrogacy agency. I would often stay on my brother's couch a couple nights a week for relief from the three-hour drive each way. My best friend would take care of my boys while I stayed with my brother. I was blessed to have her in my life, and she was like a mother to my boys. She was their aunt after all, and they loved her like a mother.

It felt like more Divine intervention when I found a house only three blocks from my brother. I believe my grandmother was at work from the other side. She always wanted us to be closer both physically and emotionally. It took a long time for everything to synchronize for me to find the right house; one I could afford and was close to work. When I walked into this house, I immediately got chills, it felt like home. My brother was with me and we both fell in love with it at first view. It was such a beautiful 1920's building, so adorable, and close to my brother! I was hooked. The managing company said there were several applications and I felt defeated. I was so in love with this place, and I had to have it. We put in our application with my brother co-signing. We got the call the next day. Our application was accepted over a number of other applicants! I was beyond excited and deep in my soul believe this was once again a serendipitous moment, another nudge from my many ancestors above.

The day my oldest and youngest sons and I moved to this beautiful house in Los Angeles that Spirit had led me too and orchestrated me acquiring will forever be etched in my mind. Dad had left me the mobile home in the mountains, and I was able to sell it, having a little extra money for my move and savings. All our stuff in the trailer needed to be packed plus there were a lot of other things to be done in order to leave. My best friend helped me with this transition so much. I was working full-time in L.A. and unable to take time off. She packed and took care of all the little things I needed to do before leaving the mountains I had called home for so long. We said goodbye to my middle son who was off to the army and with teary goodbyes left my best friend as we drove away headed to our new home. We were all excited for this new adventure, leaving the trailer park, dark moments and memories behind. Knowing a fresh start was before us, we felt lighter and were looking forward to this new part of our lives.

Little did I know there was a lot happening around me in the cosmic ethers. The synchronicities that started unfolding were and still are mind blowing. I believe the death of my dad, meeting my daughter and my suicide attempt were events carefully mobilized for karmic endings and beginnings, and I was ready. I graduated from Life Level 1 to the beginning of my new life. I was forty-five. Adding four and five of my age revealed the number nine and in numerology your life repeats or ends cycles every nine years. I was entering a new rhythm with a fresh new life. When I started as Intake Coordinator/Case Manager, I was in a number one year for me. I was on top of the world, and ready for this change. Little Girl Julie was finally getting noticed in a positive way. Others were seeing my potential, as I always knew deep inside, I was capable of. My dreams were coming true because of the growth within myself; growth I had worked so hard to obtain and come through so much for. And I was ready for this next chapter. Or at least I thought I was. This next life level had a lot of emotional ties to break. There were relationships needing to be severed, healed and forgiven. It was time to pay karmic debts and plant seeds for the future. I was starting to finally see the moments of my life coming together, the whys were being answered, healing was in process and the future was bright.

For five years I thrived as the Intake Coordinator/Case Manager. I was helping others, much like I had been helped. At the same time, I was helping and healing myself. Many meaningful hours and days were spent with my brother. Childhood wounds were healing for both of us. This was a magical time on all levels of my being. Later I would realize and understand the depth of soul restoration we both experienced and how special these years were for us.

I believe my grandma and dad had their hands in all these little steps of reinstalling nuggets of love and forgiveness along the way. Like being shown by Universe a route that allowed me to move so close to my brother during the time I needed him most. The first couple of years were a magical time. I was finding my footing in my new job; I spent almost every day with my brother after work. We became best friends during this time.

After he left at age seventeen, he went on to become a dancer and later a choreographer and self-made business owner of his own production company. He fought his way out of our dark toxic childhood and made a life he was not only successful at but proud of.

Midway through his life he made the decision to move from dance production to becoming an interior designer. Not just any interior designer but an extremely successful one to the stars. I am so proud of him, and the bond we now share is beyond anything I could have ever imagined.

He was always an anchor in my life, rescuing me through the darkness and pulling me back when I needed it most. Those challenging moments were necessary, leading me to a place where we could reconnect once more. Now being able to live three blocks from him was joyous for me. I was in awe; we grew closer and closer talking and healing which to this day has changed the maps of our lives. He influenced my future, and I influenced his in the best ways. The bond I held so close when I was eight years old has now come back to me.

My youngest son started eighth grade when we moved to L.A. My oldest son started working for my brother at his design company; he was also into music production and spinning EDM music. Moving to the entertainment capital of the world allowed him to find undergrounds to play in, which at first was great but also opened the door to some dark things to enter. I mean he was my son, right? The partying lifestyle of the night life unfortunately started to take hold of him. He began not showing up for work and doing things that were out of character for him. His path was getting darker and darker which led me to make a hard decision to kick him out of the house. This was unfathomable to me because I always said I would never do this to any of my children, but I knew deep inside if I continued to enable him things would only get worse. He left that night, and I was terrified for him. I didn't know where he would go, and I knew all too well what happened living on the streets. All the worries and fears from the time I spent on the streets came to the surface and tried to knock me off my upward path. Feelings of inadequacy flooded back, making me doubt my ability to make good decisions, while in my head, I knew this was best for him. Logically I understood my actions were necessary, but my heart ached while fear tried to strangle me. I watched him struggle for a while and saw less and less of him. Thankfully, he eventually found his way out of that darkness.

He found the love of his life, they had my beautiful grandbaby, got married and he enrolled in the Navy all within a two-year period. I am grateful for his strength and for my bravery to do what I did because it pushed him into the life he has today. One where he is successful with a beautiful wife and two wonderful daughters.

My boss was a great teacher, mentor, and father figure for me. He taught me to believe in myself, he showed me my worth and he was tough. He loved me like a daughter, and I soaked it up. He was filling a hole in the deepest part of me where Little Julie had been waiting for her loving, caring dad to appear. I helped build the company, always taking on more, and wanting to prove myself. There was no way to know this would be my downfall. The person who suggested the position to me, my surrogate intake coordinator, would also play a part in my downfall. I now believe she; my father figure boss and I had a deep karmic connection and debt that needed to be paid in this lifetime. Spending time together as a work family opened up old wounds for me. In a way I was reliving the traumas of this lifetime and remembering deep dark gashes in my soul accumulated over many lifetimes.

My boss was not only nice and showed love to me, but he was also very hard, and abusive verbally pushing me to my best but in a toxic way. I understand now that it was necessary to add my friend who got me the job to this pressurized situation. She was placed in my life to help me use my voice, speak my truth and grow into the best version of myself. It was extremely difficult to navigate at the time as I did not have the knowledge to work out what and why things were happening the way they were. I was in an awakening process without enough tools to guide me. The pressure of this job plus the karmic relationships with both of them started taking a toll on me. I didn't realize this until it was too late.

During the five years at this job that I loved, there were very good moments, and a lot of proving myself to everyone but me. I was already convinced of my capability and worth. Then little by little, layer by layer things changed and distrust began whispering in my ear. Distrust in myself, my skills as a vital member of the surrogacy placement team and distrust in my ability to be a good mother. The relationship with my youngest started taking a turn for the worse, our fighting only contributed to my downward spiral. The stress of the job and trying to raise him through the fighting and strain was beginning to be too much for me. As always, I just pushed it down and did what I needed to survive. Lifelong habits jumped right back in and repeated what I had so much experience in. I went back to hiding when things got too hard to deal with. Drinking helped camouflage me physically and emotionally. What was happening?

I was hanging on by my fingertips, breathing raggedly, wide eyed and scared to death. I was living in this dream house in a very established and well-known neighborhood just three blocks from my brother. Our relationship was exciting and deep and real. I was on top of the world. I was making more money than I could have ever dreamed of, receiving raises every year, along with bonuses and even a company car, a Lexus then a Jaguar. This is what life was all about. I wasn't the little white trash girl who was homeless and did drugs on these same streets. I was now thriving and literally living the dream. I honestly thought I had made it.

Eventually the pressure to be perfect and succeed became too heavy. I could feel myself slipping, barely holding my head above water. I was losing myself, and my self-worth was being threatened. In this supposed happy successful life, I was slowly drowning. Arguments with my son were like two teenaged rivals screaming at each other. I had no parenting skills, I had no coping skills to handle a rebellious son or the pressure and demands that came with my job, and no voice to ask for help. I didn't know how to use my voice without feeling I would upset someone and possibly lose my job. There was much I wanted to say and stick up for myself about but couldn't at that time; I hadn't learned how to communicate clearly, honestly and with conviction. Unable to maintain eye contact while voicing my opinion left the door open for them to step in, talk over me and disregard what I said. More and more was being asked of me on the job and I felt I had no option as I wasn't being seen or heard (again).

It seemed as though I had to prove myself over and over again day after day. Nervous about stepping forward I couldn't answer questions directly and was afraid if I said what I really thought I would be fired. I had gone through so much and worked hard to be in what I considered this dream life, the fear of losing what I had attained muted me. The learned way to feel better and cope resurfaced, and I started drinking again. I was so afraid of looking like a failure that I couldn't show anyone the truth. I was hiding behind the curtain concealing the scared lost little girl I had allowed to come back in control. Instead of stepping forward with shoulders back and chin up in my power, Little Julie showed herself as best she could. In fear of losing all this success that honestly felt better than anything in my life so far, I took on more work to prove myself to my boss, to make him proud so I could feel accomplished and accepted by my father figure. But this girl didn't have the skills to speak up for herself or handle the building pressures of strained relationships in fear she would lose everything. What she did know how to do, quite well actually, was rely on and gain courage through drinking, which was about to become daily, nightly and then uncontrollable. Eventually I would break, falling into the pit of an intensely difficult learning curve again.

In the midst of my internal chaos, my daughter contacted me saying she was moving to Hollywood with her boyfriend and would be living a few miles away from me. I was beyond excited and was looking forward to learning everything about her. It was hard to believe I had my brother three blocks away, and now my daughter would be close also. The relationship with my brother was perfect, we would hang out every weekend, healing our past and just BE with each other. I was ecstatic that my daughter would be close to add to our family times as we also got to know each other better.

This was the highlight of my time in Los Angeles. To have my brother back in my life and be such a huge part of it meant everything. He was proud of me, my boys were proud of me, my daughter was close, and we were learning about our relationship and love for each other. All the while I was slowly dying on the

101

inside. I loved my job, I loved living in L.A., but the pressure to keep up with the outside society was eventually going to break me.

The relationship with my daughter became very close, very fast. We spent every day together and after a bit I helped get her a job at the company I was working for. We became best friends, and I was in love with her. She was the beauty I couldn't see in myself, and the way she loved me unconditionally helped me immensely. She was perfect. Such a beautiful deep soul but I could see the pain behind it all. She struggled like me, we were so much alike it was scary. I felt pain and guilt start to recede but then our relationship became toxic because we were both full of scars. We were trying to heal by filling ourselves with each other. We did a lot of partying and drinking together. The L.A. lifestyle was great for an addict. Bottomless Mimosas on Sundays. Skinny Margaritas at El Coyote at least three nights a week and happy hour after work. It didn't take long for me to start using drugs again. First, cocaine, then Adderall, then speed. This was not my finest moment, and it broke my heart and shattered my self-worth.

Here we go again. I fell back into that same pattern of trying to cope when the feelings of worthlessness, guilt and shame so easily kept appearing in my life. I was in a cycle that needed to be broken.

Life was moving way too fast. My youngest was starting down the same path I took, not thriving in school, smoking marijuana and rebelling against me. I didn't know how to be a mom to a teenager, I didn't know how to be an executive at a company, I didn't know how to love my daughter who I gave up years ago. I didn't know how to deal with any of the stress that was building those five years, so I kept drinking and using drugs trying to relieve the pressure of maintaining the façade. I had built the currently unachievable good image I was portraying to everyone around me. I was drowning and not telling anyone.

Trying to be a good mother to my son without good role models to pull from, I found myself leaning on what I knew. Doing things and having reactions like my dad did raising me. I was repeating patterns without even realizing it. All I wanted was for my son to succeed and us become close again. Instead, the opposite was happening.

I couldn't see it in the moment, but I was continuing generational toxic traits of abuse by having a strict dictator mentality, not listening to him and insisting on "my way or the highway" which backfired and caused a tremendous amount of resentment on both sides. We were both pushing, which drove him further away. By expecting him to be what I wanted instead of his true self he rebelled even more and started to hate me.

This, my job, my boss, my coworker, my daughter, trying to live up to what everyone thought was perfect Julie, was spiraling me down bit by bit. Keeping the mask on to everyone else, but especially for myself, made me slowly start to crumble.

This made no sense! What was I doing? Why was I doing all the wrong things to bring problems to myself? I had it all, right? The perfect job, I was reunited with my daughter, living in L.A., making a lot of money, looking fancy on the outside with nice cars, a nice wardrobe and place to live but I was actually dying on the inside. UGH. I was miserable. I lost my sense of who I was, caught up in a world of dishonesty.

"Who am I? What do I really want?" I wanted to scream out loud. I wanted someone to hear me and most of all I wanted to be able to speak my truth to my boss, my coworker and my family but I couldn't. Back came the same feelings of Little Julie. The pain of not being seen or heard. I don't know if it showed on the outside but inside, I was pulling my shoulders in and up trying to protect myself from what didn't feel good as I had in school, trying to protect myself from the bullies and the fear. I felt myself spiraling, I was losing control but didn't know how to stop the descent. It took years for me to understand I was causing my own breakdown because I didn't yet know I was truly worthy of all the good things that were in my life right then. My belief system was stuck in the past where the truth was poor Little Julie had a rough life and wasn't good enough. I didn't know what self-sabotage was, but I was learning that lesson the hard way.

Spirituality was only tapped into when I was using speed once a weekend or during a full moon. How horrible. Who was I? Growing quiet I became increasingly impatient with others and myself. Inside I was jittery as I felt more and more trapped. Drugs had always been my savior. I knew I could depend on how they made me feel, going into the numbness was so appealing. All the while I knew in my logical brain drugs were going to be what broke me. I knew I was going to fall, and I didn't know how to stop it.

Work was failing because our team was not functioning as a unit any longer. I wasn't able to speak the truth to my boss and coworker which possibly would have gotten us back on track. Then suddenly it happened; on came my first emotional breakdown and it was a big one.

We had a team meeting at work to help us bond and work better as a group. We ordered food and alcohol as I requested. Everyone was there and we sat around the big conference table supposedly waiting to say what was needed from each of us to clear the air.

Previously all my coworkers had come to me separately to share how they felt about others in the office and what they thought was wrong with the business. I seemed to be the unofficial office confidant. I knew how each of them felt and I was under the impression we were all going to participate in an open discussion on what we thought was needed in order for us to move forward. Little did I know no one would come clean. My boss was pleased, thinking everyone was happy. I knew the truth and was waiting and expecting the gates to open.

One of them finally decided to let it out. This person had learned to push my buttons over these last few years and now started in on me, throwing me under the bus, about what I can't remember, but I can remember the feelings boiling up inside me like a volcano ready to explode. My daughter, who knew how I truly felt, and the other three coworkers were all looking at each other not knowing what to say. It was beyond awkward. I was enraged and didn't care who I hurt or what I said in that moment. I was drunk, and I was falling.

Right then and there I had a fiery nervous breakdown. Livid, hurt and in disbelief of what just happened, I finally said what I needed to say to every single person in that room. Blowing up and getting everything off my chest, saying exactly what, I honestly don't know, but admittedly in the wrong way. Words were just pouring out of me and tears were flowing from my eyes. I stormed out shaking, crying and hyperventilating. The things I said would be the downfall of the position I had loved so much, taking with it all the successes of my life at that time. I left the Intake Coordinator/Case Manager role shortly after that explosion, within two days of my five-year company anniversary.

Later the lesson came to me: speak your truth every day, stand up for yourself and know your worth. Don't allow someone else to define you.

After my breakdown, I was placed on disability which thankfully protected me financially. This was a lifesaver, and I took full advantage of it. I started therapy with both a therapist and psychiatrist and was placed on several medications. There was talk of a possible diagnosis of bi-polar illness but that never became official. I did everything possible to figure it out and get a diagnosis of what was wrong with me, but never once did I think I had a drinking problem. Funny how our brain can cover up something when it feels we need it. I knew I had an issue with drugs. That was obvious. In the beginning of my disability, and added medications, I was still using speed and drinking a lot. I was in shock, cold, numb, felt like I weighed a ton and dizzy, not sleeping enough or too much. Waves of realization had me vacillating between relief, embarrassment and empowerment as I understood and felt my way through the fact that my whole world, which I had lovingly worked hard to build, was all crumbling. Everything was gone in an instant, my security, my foundation and my identity. My world was cracking wide open, allowing and pushing me to take a deep look at myself, my views of who I was, what I believed and who I wanted to become.

Also, the relationship with my daughter started to disintegrate during this time. The partying and the drinking were taking their toll on both of us and the foundation we had quickly built on those crutches was unraveling, becoming very shaky. I remember telling her if she ever told anyone about the partying we did together, I couldn't handle it. I felt it would be the end of who I was, as a human and a mother because a good mother would have tried to shield her daughter rather than participate in that lifestyle. Shortly that is exactly what happened and my world turned upside down again.

We had planned a trip up to the mountains (where I live now) to celebrate our daddies and spend some time together. We were both excited about this trip and we were looking forward to sharing this special time together. She was dating someone and started sharing a lot about our relationship, a lot about me. He talked her out of going on the trip with me and planted the seed that our relationship was toxic and not normal.

To this day, I am glad this happened but, in that moment, I thought it was the end of my world. I see now it was all part of the bigger plan, a plan I was unable to see right then. All I could see was my relationship with my daughter was ending, my world was crumbling and everything I feared was about to be on the front page of our family newsletter.

My youngest son and I ended up going on the trip to remember my dad's death and spread some of his ashes on the mountain he loved so much. I was drunk the entire time and was in a state of depression that the alcohol just fueled. I was drunk, my usual self at the time, and made him drive for the first time which was about a two-and-a-half-hour trip one way. Thinking back now, I realize what a tragedy it was for him to see me in that condition and take care of me that day. So many bad things could have happened to us. I could have killed my son, and others, by allowing him to drive with no experience on the mountain road, and on the busy freeways. Thanks to our guides and angels and most likely my dad, we made it home safe but not after I yelled at him and made him feel like shit, causing wounds I would later regret. Not a good weekend, and not a good time for my son either.

My drinking was getting out of control again. I was living a lie, protecting the amount I drank from my therapist, my family and even myself.

Shortly after that horrendous mountain trip, I blew up my life once again. I found out my daughter told her boyfriend all about me and our relationship. He convinced her to distance herself from me and she started pulling away. My world started tumbling. I now know I was on too many prescribed medications for depression, anxiety and sleep disorder because I wasn't being truthful. Plus, self-medicating with whatever would work including illegal drugs and booze to suppress what was happening. I thought if I could feel better, things would be better.

Early in life I was taught drugs were a normal thing to do when you were stressed or bored, giving me those coping mechanisms at such a young age. I was taught by my dad that it was okay, even a normal way to deal with life. I repeatedly told myself, since my dad did it, and he could stop using on his own, so could I and I wasn't an addict or an alcoholic.

On this particular night, my daughter and I got into an argument. My son was out with friends. I was scared of what was happening within and about the failing relationship with my daughter. Home alone except for my trusty friends, drugs and vodka. The more I drank the worse I got, and I decided I couldn't live like this anymore. I just wanted to go to sleep, I was so tired of the charade. Not thinking of anyone but myself, a long sleep seemed the way to fix it all.

I took a handful of pills (Ativan) and continued to drink and drink and drink. I later found out I did a group text with my son and daughter without even knowing. That is how messed up I was. I am grateful I did because the next thing I remember was waking up in the hospital.

Seemingly I had tried to take my life but that wasn't my intention. I was at my bottom simply trying to rest and get relief. I just couldn't handle all the emotions and feelings coming from losing my dream, my daughter and son, job, self-esteem and my way in life.

My secrets were about to be told to my whole family. While I was unconscious in the hospital, my daughter told my other children and brother about all the drugs and partying I had been doing over the past year. The heavy cloak I had been wearing was torn off and the door of the closet I was in was thrown open. My worst fear came true, everyone was seeing me as a failure. I spent 72 hours on suicide watch in a mental hospital. I don't blame her for telling, I am actually glad she did, because it was such a relief afterwards, when my healing started.

My oldest son came up from San Diego and my middle son took time off work, both helping care for me and my youngest son while I was in the hospital. I was and am beyond grateful for both of them, and at the same time, I hold deep regret that they had to take care of me in such a dark time. I can't believe I did this again to my kids. My children pulled together to help me, and it warmed my heart.

I hope all my children know the actions I took were never about them or because of my lack of love for them; they are the greatest and best parts of me. The absence of healthy life training and the huge hole within was what drove me. I am sorry the abuse of my childhood affected my children. The trauma I caused all my children tugs at my heart even to this day. I know they forgive me, but I also know they will be dealing with that sorrow and grief as they live their lives. My deepest wish was and is to see all of them break free and thrive. I am deeply thankful I am here to witness them as happy flourishing adults now.

This whole ordeal led me, and I found out later, my daughter into our healing journeys. She moved back to Oregon with her mother and became sober within a few months. This makes me feel relieved and eternally happy. Even though we still don't talk, I hope she has found forgiveness for me in her heart. She is thriving and living her best life through her substance-free recovery path. That is all I want for her.

That 72-hour hospital hold would have probably been longer, but I had previously planned a trip to Sedona, Arizona for a shamanic healing retreat. For some reason I was released. The only logical explanation, at least logical to me and those who believe in Divine intervention, is that my Guides arranged it. My brother really wanted me to go but my boys didn't. They were scared and worried that it wasn't a good idea to travel on my own after such a major event, but I was determined. I knew it was exactly what I needed, spiritual healing, and it was time.

My ultimate goal for the retreat was to heal for my children and become the mother I needed to be for them. I stopped drinking and felt alive for the first time in a very long time. Sedona was beyond anything I expected. I did some deep healing and was told through an intuitive message that I had a drinking problem and should attend some type of 12 step program. I was still in denial. I believed I could stop on my own, and when I wanted, I could drink like any other person.

Sedona had much more to offer than I expected. My teacher was amazing and he was the first person I didn't hold back with, telling him the truth about addictions, my children and how I was living my life. Maybe this is why he made the statement, "you do have a drinking problem, and need more help than you are telling yourself." He knew what he was talking about and so did my spiritual team who had been guiding me towards help that I hadn't accepted. He gave me a book to read that would be a huge influence on changing my pattern of dysfunctional thinking. It was called "Somebody should have told us. Simple truths to living well" by Jack Pransky. This book was the first thing that actually made sense to me, something I could grab hold of and use moving forward on my healing journey.

The fact that I was let out of the hospital early to go on this trip was definitely orchestrated by my guides and ancestors. I spent time in the vortexes, released dark energy that was attached to me, and opened myself up more than I had ever before. The experience was eye opening and mind blowing. Feelings were overwhelming but in a good way. I felt loved by the Universe and myself while feeling connected to Source and this Earth-bound life much more than ever before. This experience would plant seeds that I could have never thought possible. The experiences were profound and changed my soul and consciousness. Suddenly I had an understanding of ancestral trauma, and how we pass this down generation to generation. I felt on fire and truly alive for the first time in a very long time. I saw the light finally and believed I was on the path to healing myself, my trauma, and becoming the mother my children needed. This euphoria and feeling of being a new person lasted quite a while.

A few months later, in the middle of a worldwide pandemic, I finally concluded I have a drinking problem, and all my issues stem from alcohol. That's when my healing journey towards sobriety began. Alcohol is my gateway drug that opens the door for all other substances in my life. Covid, isolation, and getting involved with "friends" who helped me bottom out forcing me to face my life head on, would be the end of the struggle in my life. All the dots connected for me to figure out how to save myself.

Shortly after the 2020 pandemic engulfed the world, I decided it was a good idea to move and help some people I considered friends at the time build their cannabis industry. This sounded like such a great idea at the time, as I was not working, on unemployment and just looking for a quick fix to my situation. I loved this friend and her family. They had been there for me for quite a few years, and I considered her whole family my family. I lost Me within her world as I witnessed her living a so-called normal life, while drinking and using other substances occasionally. She had a beautiful home, family and lots of friends. They had built a successful business, and I soon would be a part of that. It felt right, and she helped me move back to the place I left six years ago in the mountains which I loved.

I immersed myself in their life. They included me in their group functions, supplying what I had been searching for all my life; a kind network of people offering what seemed like caring from a family unit. I believed they were good people, prospering, doing everything I wanted to do. I never once saw their actions as trauma playing out.

What I saw was successful, in my eyes, people doing well while drinking and using so I told myself it was okay, and I could do that too. All my life I watched my dad and others show how by example. Even if I had an issue with alcohol, I could still do all the other stuff and as long as I kept a handle on drinking, I would be fine. Not only fine but making connections that would benefit me in many ways, at least that's what I kept telling myself. Afterall my friends were using in different ways, and they had it all together with their own business and they were thriving. I was fortunate that they wanted me to become involved and help expand the business and myself, right? My father taught me as long as you have success, stability and are holding it together it's all good. When I saw others functioning normally using and drinking, I believed it was okay for me too. I assumed, wrongly, if they were doing it and living a good life then it would be good for me as well.

Feeling loved and cared for as a member of the family, I allowed myself to get deep into my friend's trauma. I permitted her actions to become a part of me, going against my integrity, helping her lie and achieve her goals while I lived in pain. The pain of guilt from lying, pain of being manipulated by a friend, pain from doing and saying things I knew were wrong. It was a dark time that I didn't see as such because I loved her, and I wanted to be a part of and help build her happiness. It became a huge lesson in choosing people to be in my life.

Because I was unwell, I chose unwell people to be around when they treated me in a way I was craving. I still believe part of the family who were sober really cared about me, but my friend needed a scapegoat, someone to manipulate and cover for her. I desperately needed a friend, I loved her and how she and the rest of the family made me feel, filling a huge void inside me. My integrity became blurred, and I forgot who I was and what I believed in. I paid a heavy price for this. Believe, me it could have been way worse, and I could have killed someone. Thank God for my Guides' protection and my karma. The only one who paid the price for this mistake was me. Don't get me wrong, her family also paid the price, but through her actions and her karma, not because of me. This was another karmic debt relationship; heavy, hard, surrounded with great rewards, meant for my growth and change. I see this now. As I have since learned, no part of that lifestyle is good for me, and it isn't a place where I can thrive. In fact, it is a place that will slam me down and take away everything I hold dear, including myself.

I am thankful for these *friends* who helped me during this time. I really cherished our friendship, and the acceptance of the whole family, always including me in all the big family functions. If I had not felt part of a loving family that I could take my guard down with, I would likely not have gotten so involved in drinking and using again and I know now I needed to be in that place to take me to the next place and the next that would ultimately release me. They were part of my journey, illuminating all the dark parts that needed to fall away in order for me to wake up and make the change to finally do something for me, not to hide behind the alcohol and drugs anymore.

The next year, my life would end up taking a turn that would be another dark and scary moment, but it would also be the light at the end of the tunnel that would end up waking me up and saving me.

I had a dream of the impending doom that was headed my way. I told everyone about it, but no one believed me. In great detail my dream foretold the loss of the house and the business we were building. Five months later the dream unfolded in the current time and space confirming one of my spiritual abilities. All of it came true, almost exactly as my dream showed.

I was about to lose everything again. But this time would be the moment I finally saw the truth of who I was, and who I didn't want to be anymore.

Part Three

# The Bloom

*"And when the dawn warms earth and air, the rose will bloom, beyond despair.*

*A light of hope through life's darkest groom, I find my life's constant bloom."*

The *friend* I had been so close to and manipulated by and another friend decided to take a trip to Colorado. We had been lying to our families about so much it didn't seem to matter if we lied about where we were going or what we would be doing. We took this trip without telling our families so we could play and have fun-translate *to drink and use drugs without having to hide or explain ourselves*. We had been concealing our true actions for quite a while and wanted freedom. She had been cheating on her husband and we both had been lying about our substance abuse. It seemed like a good idea and then it wasn't. Everything seemed good on the drive to Colorado. We were excited to break free and of course we were drinking, always drinking.

We had just finished having dinner and drinks at a beautiful restaurant. I was intoxicated but nothing more than 'normal' for me, so driving didn't seem that big of a deal. But this fateful night, the universe had something else in mind for me.

Drinking and driving was the norm for me, I didn't have a problem therefore I could drink whenever I wanted, I told myself. The fact that I thought I could get away with this and have no implications for my actions still blows my mind. I was driving on mountain roads with my girlfriend and her friend and had a car accident. I am grateful for only injuring myself in the accident. Both of my friends walked away without a scratch. Talk about being lucky. I was badly hurt and in the hospital for four days. It blows my mind I still didn't believe I had a problem. I left the hospital with even more medication, adding Ativan and pain pills to what I was already taking.

My entire life I had a pre-knowing, but I didn't realize it was about to manifest in my waking life. I had this recurring dream of driving off a mountain road and down a cliff. That is exactly what happened on that night.

The dream I had throughout my life was playing out RIGHT NOW! It's hard to say whether I blacked out before or after hitting the guard rail and driving off the ninety-foot cliff. I woke up pinned and trapped in the driver's seat. I could hear my friends calling "Julie, are you okay?" Over and over. I was out of it, and stuck. I couldn't move.

I was hanging upside down in a mangled car. Rescuers cut me out of the car with the jaws of life and carried me up the 90-foot cliff to the road. Thank God my friends, who were not wearing their seatbelts, were not even touched, not injured in any way, a miracle indeed. I was and am beyond grateful that it wasn't far worse. I believe this accident was part of my life plan as a wakeup call by literally turning my world upside down.

At that time, I didn't even realize I was spiraling deeper and deeper into the abyss hiding behind what I considered an okay life. Oblivious to all the warning signs, I was swirling headfirst towards the same ultimate relief I had learned from my mom. Death.

While I was in the hospital the cops came and drew blood for testing. I had done cocaine that day and night, as well as drinking all day. At that moment, I didn't care how the blood test came out. I was in so much pain, receiving treatments for three broken ribs, injured left thigh, internal bleeding requiring a blood transfusion and staples in my head.

I was pretty banged up, but not dead. Thank God. To this day, I have a lump and deformity on my left upper leg. A funny thing to note is when I was younger and did my natal chart, it mentioned later in life I might get an injury that would cause some type of deformity if I didn't keep my life on track. Not a coincidence. After leaving Colorado, I knew I was going to get a DUI charge but for some reason I didn't let it affect me. I think because it was out of state, I thought everything would be ok, I could run away from my problems again. After the accident, I still drank and continued on all the other medications I was on.

When we got back home after the accident, I stayed with my *friend* for a few weeks so she could help me get around and she felt safe at that time. I clung to her even more because I was scared and felt like I was on the losing side of things again. Our families had found out the truth about all the things: drugging, excessive drinking, her cheating, both of us covering for the other and our lying. My children were devastated to find out I had been far from honest with them but glad I was safe. Her marriage was suffering, and I was caught between trying to keep a friend and my own integrity. I knew things were getting worse. We both knew our families were extremely upset with us, and that made our bond stronger. We were together, covering the other's back, through the lies and dysfunction. I was pretty much checked out during this time. My thoughts weren't clear, I was drug and alcohol dazed and had no idea what was in store for me. I drank more to numb more.

A few months later I decided to rent an Air BNB in the local mountains for some soul searching and time to write. I stayed four days, alone, just digging deep within myself. I found out I was being charged with a second DUI and started the process on the case. Life in general was still upside down and weird with the pandemic, so I was allowed to do video court in the beginning. Synchronistic moments like this were leading me to where I am today. My sobriety.

I did a lot of writing during my four days, along with a lot of soul searching, and I really felt like I was in a good place. STILL DRINKING though but starting to work on my soul and self. I was still seeing my psychiatrist and taking all my depression meds, anxiety meds and sleeping meds while drinking. I feel like the first part of 2021 led into the year that began the end of who Julie was and who Julie was becoming. It all makes sense to me now. Each orchestrated moment from the accident to the healing session in the mountains, then to the end of the cannabis business and the change in my living situation.

I had to go to court twice, once for the arraignment and then for my sentencing. The arraignment went well, and I thought the sentencing would be the same. In the months after my accident, things started to deteriorate with my misidentified *friends*. Our business and drinking and using became the main focus as we tried to deal with all the stress of our circumstances. In May, our landlords did a walk thru, found our grow house, and we were evicted. I had seen this part of our downfall in the dream I mentioned earlier. I had one month to find a place and pick myself up. I found a place in the little town where I had secluded myself earlier, and we were ready to move to our new place the day before my court date. I had everything planned for my son to move us while I was gone. I hired movers, packed the house, and made sure he was taken care of, or at least I thought I did. I was drinking and using with another friend to cope and get through this major shift and change. She ended up going with me to Colorado for my court date. I had no idea what would happen next, and it changed my life beyond anything I ever expected.

The night before my court date was perfectly calculated and set in place by the Universe. What happened became THE reason behind me wanting to get sober, wanting to change. It would tug at my core in the worst possible way. The friend who went to support me in court and I had been drinking on the plane, on the drive to the hotel, and then we were off to dinner and more drinks. That night was a blur. I had just been enjoying my time, my drinking, and at that point had not even cared about what my son was going through with the move. I was so caught up in Julie, and partying before my court tomorrow nothing else mattered. After dinner, and of course more drinks, we ended up in the downtown center just talking to people. I was on cloud nine, without a care in the world and found a group of teenagers I wanted to talk with.

After four hours of talking with them, as if they wanted to hang out with a fifty-two year old mother, something happened. Something that would change my life forever. What happened was never my intention or what I was trying to portray but it happened anyway. My intoxication demolished my boundaries, and I made someone feel threatened, scared and violated. This was never my intention, of course, and in that moment, I didn't even realize what had happened. As I was leaving, or walking to another bar, I was approached by cops and interviewed by them. I was in shock at what they were saying about me. My experience was much different than the accounts of the teens I was with. In that moment I blew it off because I knew deep inside what they were accusing me of was a lie. I could never do such a thing, not me! I knew in my core I didn't do what I was being accused of, but I was also extremely intoxicated, and the lines were blurred. Even after my accident and the fact I was going to court the next morning for a DUI didn't phase me. I didn't have a drinking problem, did I?

I woke the next morning with a severe hangover and began drinking a hard seltzer to help. I had to be in court in less than 2 hours and I was dying. I remembered the night before my son had called me, and there was an issue with the movers, and all I can remember was I didn't give a shit. I basically ignored my son, and what he was going through. I couldn't even remember the full conversation, or what issue he was having. I was again caught up in my own fucked up world.

I arrived at court on time, and just wanting it to be over so I could go eat and drink more. Little did I know I was about to be sidelined in the worst way imaginable. As I stood there before the judge, listening to her and accepting charges, all I heard was "I am sentencing you to forty days in jail." What? OMG, what did she just say? In that moment, I lost everything. I was scared beyond anything I could ever imagine, and I was going to jail. Me? How could this be happening? I had no idea and felt like my lawyer fucked me. I was devastated. The sheriff put handcuffs on me, I gave my friend all the cash I had for the rental car. The sheriff walked me to the back of the courtroom and placed me in a holding cell.

In shock I waited to be transported to jail. In another state, alone, scared and feeling like my life was over I called my son, and what happened next shattered my world even more than I thought possible. He basically told me he hated me; he knew I was out drinking the night before and when he needed me, I wasn't there, I didn't care. He said he was glad I was going to jail and said he was embarrassed I was his mother. I lost it, broke down and felt totally defeated. I was hitting rock bottom and for the first time, I knew he was right, and I knew alcohol was the issue. I remember thinking 'This isn't who Julie is, or who I want to be.' Scared Little Julie was crying out, searching and looking in all the wrong places just wanting to be saved. All my worst fears were coming true and in that moment all the moments from January to this day flashed in front of me. I could see

126

the synchronicities, and how they all lined up perfectly to bring me to this moment. The moment where I had to humble myself, and only had me to lean on, to figure out how to change somehow, someway. I was determined to no longer be an embarrassment to my children, to my friends or to myself.

Jail was one place I always told myself I would never go because I was too good for it. I didn't have a drinking problem because I didn't go to jail, I wasn't hurting anyone. I didn't have a drug problem because I had never been in jail. Then shockingly to me because I didn't have a problem, I was sitting there, humiliated, lost, confused and scared. Terrified to be honest. I called my son again, and once again all he did was yell at me, scream at me, telling me I deserved everything I got, and how he hated me. I deserved all of it. He began to tell me what happened when he called the night before. How I hung up on him when he needed me most. How sad, and how sorry I am for ever being that person. That was not who I was deep inside. Inside was the lost, scared little girl just wanting to be loved, and saved. I was beginning to understand no one was going to save me but me! Everything I learned over the years with my spiritual endeavors was all in front of me at this moment. It all was starting to make sense through a group of moments put in motion for me to be in this one spot. The spot that would become my light at the end of a dark and lonely tunnel.

During the first week in jail, I slept 95% of the time. I was put on a five-day detox program taking valium tapering off over the five days, so I was very groggy and of course depressed. On day three, I was called into a room, where I was met by an officer. We sat down, and he began to tell me a story that blew my mind. I could not comprehend what he was saying, and knew these accusations against were not true. I was groggy so it was hard to understand what he was saying but basically, I was being charged with unlawful touching of a minor while hanging out with the teenagers the night before court. In my head I dismissed the charges because I knew what they were saying wasn't true, and it was never my intention.

What I did know was I had been drunk and everything about that night was a blur. I went before a judge for arraignment on those charges while in jail. My bail was set at $3000 cosigner bond which meant I could only be released if someone in the state of Colorado would sign for me and place $3000 for my bail. I had forty days to serve and work on the bond but let me tell you that was one of the hardest things for me to process and I thought I was never going to be released. It was not my finest moment, but it was the moment that changed my life for the better. All these perfect synchronicities lined up for my highest good.

On the fifth day in jail, I wasn't so groggy anymore and I picked up the AA Big Book and started reading it from page one. I read it in three days and was blown away. I saw myself on every page in that book. I saw I had a drinking and drug problem; it was my escape since I was a very young girl. I had become what I was taught by my father and programmed to believe that drinking and drugging is normal, how you relieve stress, and cope.

After reading the Big Book I was on a mission. My mind was clear, and I was determined to win back the love and trust of my son and everyone in my life including myself. I was determined to fight the current charges and not allow it to ruin my life. I ended up spending twenty-seven days in jail of the forty-day sentence on two charges. By the grace of my brother, Angels, Guides and Ancestors a miracle happened to have me released.

The events that led up to the instant I was released were nothing short of supernatural to say the least. I was distraught because I knew I had no way out unless someone in the state of Colorado could sign for me and that was never going to happen. My brother helped me again. He contacted his attorney, and his attorney's connections were the only reasons I was released on bond for the second charge. It all changed and happened so fast. I thought I was never getting out and was shocked to be saved and released.

Sitting in jail, I was able to work on me and get in a better place emotionally and spiritually by doing a lot of writing, manifesting, and praying. I believe in my soul my words were heard, as my brother's attorney was able to change the bond from cosigner to just $3000 bond. In that instant my life changed. I understood Divine manipulation when I found out my brother's connections to connections to connections were able to work out the bond. I was released sober for the first time since my teenage years and was on a mission to change, ready to take on the world. I had a long way to go, no job, a new home and a son who hated me but at least I was sober and willing to fight for my life.

The charge of unlawfully touching a minor hit me somewhere deep in my core. It messed with my integrity in a way I never ever wanted to be associated with. My brother once again came to my rescue and hired an amazing attorney for me. Over the next year we fought to at least get the charges dropped from a sex charge to an assault misdemeanor. Long story short, the charge was reduced to a motived bias assault, and I stood in court apologizing to the victim, the judge and myself. My oldest son went to court with me, and spent a lot of time watching me grow and change. He told me that day, how proud he was of me, and this healing journey I was on is the legacy I will leave my kids. That touched me and, in that moment, I knew this book would come to fruition and I would make my life story a testimony for my family. My goal now is to make sure I leave the legacy of healing my son envisioned.

I have been sober since the day I went to jail. They took all my medications away and I haven't been on any antidepressants or anxiety medications since that day. I remember being in panic mode fighting to get my meds while in jail. It took over two weeks for them to finally get approval. They had to check with my therapist to get proof of my current prescriptions. The meds never came and that was a true gift to me. I can still hear the social worker/therapist I was seeing in jail say these words that forever changed my mind on how I felt about all the crutches and devices I was using to numb my soul over the years. "If you can survive jail on nothing, you can survive anything." I haven't taken any medication since. I haven't needed them. No alcohol, drugs or anything that altered my once numb mind. Freedom from my addictions has now given me more strength and clarity than I have ever had before.

The accident in January, the eviction in July, court in August, charged with DUI, jail, and my new charge were all the perfect mix of circumstances that forever changed my life for the better. I always say there was a silver lining in that year because 2021 was all about loss, pain, rejection, change, redemption, and freedom. Freedom from the demons that plagued my life since I was twelve years old. Having to face those demons head on, not on my terms but on Universe's terms was a year of extremes for me. Spirit deemed it was necessary and time for the events that were needed for me to see the truth and the light at the end of a very dark tunnel. No matter what anyone else believes I know all of it was perfectly planned for my highest good. I am living a life full of peace now, working on this book and myself continuously. It is my mission to break the generational bondage our family has been plagued with and show my kids you can overcome all obstacles on your path.

After I was released from jail, I finally made it to my new home. The one I had forced my son to move into without me and without any support from me whatsoever. The place where so many bad moments happened setting into motion a huge powerful downward spiral in my life. I was back in the little mountain town where I had lived with Dad so many years ago. I had come full circle, but I did not realize it until I was driving to my new job a few weeks later.

My sobriety date is August 4, 2021, the first day I woke up in jail became the first day of my sobriety. What a long, strange trip it has been to say the least. As I look back at all the moments that led to this place in my life, I see it is a perfectly orchestrated road map to all things better. Believe me, in those moments it did not always feel like my life was actually getting better but somehow, I knew deep inside everything would be ok. It certainly didn't look or feel like that, but I had this knowing.

When I arrived home, my life was still a mess on the outside. All the things I used to drink to push down were now right in front of my face, waiting for me to deal with head on, sober, and I was going to do everything in my power to complete this mission, proving to myself that I could. I started working on getting my life better and knew it would all make sense in the end.

The relationship with my youngest was anything but good. There was so much trauma and toxicity between us, it was going to take a very long time to heal. Even to this day, I still see moments of toxic traits on both sides that were picked up over the years. Drinking, drug use, traumatic childhoods and poor parental role models had all played a part in the trauma-led parenting I did and didn't do.

The first few months we fought a lot. Therapy taught me he was still playing out the toxic cycles of fighting that were programmed within him and of course my first reaction was to engage and prove that I had changed. I learned very quickly from my new job, treatment and therapy I was attending weekly, not to engage, to let things be, the proof of my changing was in my actions, not in my words. I couldn't heal him. He had to see for himself that I had changed, he could feel safe again within my company and see that his world wasn't going to be a mess due to my actions. Don't get me wrong, I am not saying he never did anything wrong. He learned a lot of his narcissistic behaviors from me, and we were mirrors of each other, repeating cycles of dysfunction over and over again. Being sober I could finally see all that. The road for us was a long one, but it has been over two years now and we are in a much better place, I see the growth in him but mainly in myself.

My other two boys are doing great in their lives. I know my absence and crazy life during their childhood and teen years caused some scars in their hearts, but I have seen firsthand the strength they have. They have both grown into amazing young men full of potential and have made me very proud.

This is why I am writing this book. It is intended as a roadmap for my children, for others to see it is possible to heal the trauma and live a safe, happy life.

When I came home from jail, I was in the last two weeks of unemployment, my benefits were ending soon, and my goal was to find a job on the mountain asap. My youngest son's grandma, who I cherished, was in the program and had been sober for twenty plus years. I was there for her when she first got sober and now, she wanted to return the favor. She came up and stayed often, attending meetings with me, moderated fights with my son, and just helped me cope with everyday life. At one of those meetings, I met a wonderful woman who's aura stood out to me, and I was drawn to her and her husband. I was at the point in my sobriety where I needed to find a sponsor, so I was on the search for one. She stood out so brightly, and I gained the courage to go over and talk to her. What transpired next blew my mind. I shared a little of my story with her, and I learned she owned a woman's treatment center on the mountain, she loved the actress Julie Andrews and offered me a job. They were hiring a medical assistant and needed me asap. They were being bought out by another bigger company which I needed to apply to and interview with. I sent my resume, and within a week I was hired at the pay rate I requested. All within the timeline I needed as my unemployment ran out only a week before. All the planets aligned, and I was employed in a treatment center. What a blessing! She was a blessing! The people I met at this place were a blessing. I loved my job, helping others in sobriety and loved being on the front lines of it. I learned so much in that first year; about myself, my healing, my addiction and life.

One morning while driving to this job, on the beautiful mountain roads I had the epiphany that I had to come back to the mountain to heal the lost little girl who many years ago started her drug addiction on this very mountain, in this very town. As I worked the 12 steps, and wrote my step four, I began to see all of the tragic moments as blessings in disguise, how every single one of them, even the most painful ones, all made me who I am today. A victim, A survivor, A mother, An addict, An alcoholic, A friend, A beautiful soul.

Amazingly the last three years began with living at the bottom, as my life had to restart at the bottom. I still had another court case pending, possibly leading to a sexual assault conviction. I was living in a slum house, tiny, old and about to fall down but I was on cloud nine, because I was healing, sober and working at one of the best jobs yet. I felt needed and alive. I felt like I was working on myself by simply going to work. It was great. Within six months, I moved from that house to another slum house but bigger. I called it the spider house because it was full of spiders. Even with the step up in size I knew I had to get out of there as soon as I could. I started an affirmations group with my coworkers at the lodge, and every day I would ask for my dream house, among other things of course. These girls were my strength, my brightest lights during these rough times in early sobriety. Within six months of starting the affirmation group I found my dream house. It was posted on Facebook. Everyone wanted to be there too because of the beautiful mountain location. We had to do an interview with the owners, and my girls went with me. We went on our lunch break, and I fell in love with it. It was fully furnished, it had a game room with a pool table, had everything I asked for except the fenced yard. I envisioned my boys coming up, playing pool, family dinners and especially my beautiful granddaughters enjoying it with me. Plus, it was the same price I was paying for the spider house! I had to get this place. The owner interviewed several people over a two-day period, so my chances were not the greatest, but I knew in my heart it was my house. I had the same feeling I did when I walked into the house in L.A. all those years ago. It was meant to be. A couple days later I emailed her, and she replied they chose me! They chose me because she knew I would love it like it was my own, she had been a surrogate in the past, so we had that in common, and she loved my brother's work and had bought his book. The connection was undeniable.

It has been two years living here in this beautiful home, where this book grew, and the universe allowed me the dedication, time and solitude to write it. I have grown so much over these last three years; it is unthinkable as I write these pages that I am actually writing about myself. I left the treatment center and went back to creating families through surrogacy. I ended up connecting with a wonderful woman who owns an agency in Pasadena. She trusted me, gave me the freedom to work from home, and we have dedicated our time to helping many families along their journeys. I feel truly blessed to have her in my life, and in my corner. I have many close sober friends, and many spiritual friends in our local yoga community. Life is much different now.

There is peace within my relationships with my children. Especially, with my youngest who is now thriving in his life. We have healed a lot of our past issues, and I am very proud of the man he is growing into.

My middle son is also thriving in his career and relationships. I couldn't be prouder of him. He has also had many painful moments that he has worked through to conquer some very dark times. He struggled with loss in his early twenties and watching him struggle with the pain was hard to do but he has since seemed to find his way out and rise above the chains that were pulling him down and is now one year sober.

My oldest is also thriving with his beautiful wife and two precious daughters. He is now traveling through Europe as he was deployed there this year with the Navy. He has also seemed to conquer his dark moments and rise above the pain of the past.

My heart goes out to my daughter daily through my meditations as I send her love on her healing journey. My hope is we can come together through our healing and build a relationship someday.

I have dedicated these last three years, to breaking down the wall one brick at a time, one day at a time and giving myself as much grace as needed. As I mentioned before, I made a vow not to date after my last relationship in 2006, so I didn't repeat the pattern of toxic relationships around my children. I am still single but through my healing, I now feel I am ready to find a healthy and happy relationship. I am ready to move off the mountain back to society, closer to my brother and start the next major chapter in my life, helping others to heal.

Thank you, Universe, and thank you Julie for believing I deserved to be in this life space, knowing in my heart it was already mine. That is the power and miracles of the Universe.

My hope is for you to see the magic within your scars.

# Conclusion

As I write this book, I feel I have come full circle in my life, and I am ready for the next chapter to begin. This book means so much to me.

Life doesn't have to be a prison wall we build around ourselves scar after scar. Life doesn't have to be lonely; life doesn't have to be full of disappointment. Life can get better, life can surprise you, and life can be ultimately beautiful. Through all the scars, the darkness, the pain and the loss we can become warriors. I won't sit here and tell you it is easy, but I will tell you it is doable. I know you can do it because I did, but first you have to believe you can. You have to want it and want it so badly that suffering is no longer an option. You have to do the hard work, you have to fight, and you have to do it all by yourself. You will find people on your path, the universe will send you helpers, teachers and friends along the way, but it is your responsibility to fight, to learn, to grow and achieve the life you want.

I know it sounds cliché, but I am a walking testimony. No one can tell me otherwise. My journey is my journey, my experiences are my experiences and from dark to light, they are real. Just as your journey and experiences are yours alone. There is an unseen energy, call it what you want, that is waiting to assist you on your journey. I love the quote by Paulo Coelho "when you set your mind to something, the universe conspires to assist you." That is the magic. Determination to change and want more for yourself is the formula for that change. Believe in yourself so much that you learn to fall in love with all parts of you as a child, a teenager, a young adult and who you are about to become. A fucking warrior!

*The End*

# About The Author

Julie Andrews holds a Bachelor's in Metaphysical Science from Sedona University, where she also earned her certification in Spiritual Counseling. Her passion for personal growth and helping others led her to this path, and she is dedicated to guiding people on their own transcendent journeys. Her transformation thus far has planted the seed to study many religions and sacred teachings, and she hopes to start a healing practice soon.

Julie is a mother, grandmother, and surrogate mother, roles she cherishes deeply. In addition to her spiritual work, Julie has spent the past ten years in the surrogacy field as an intake counselor and coordinator working closely with both parties until the perfect match is found, offering her expertise and support every step of the way. Her experience, compassion and drive has brought her to the position of Agency Director. She works closely with new surrogates, guiding them through the process and preparing them for their passage through this part of their life. When she's not offering guidance to her surrogates or spending time writing, Julie enjoys yoga, dance, and spending time in nature, particularly the mountains where she lives. The peace and beauty of the natural world brings her a sense of calm and inspiration.

This self-help memoir is Julie's first book, created with the hope that sharing her story offers healing and encouragement to others along their own paths.